OF TIME AND SPIRIT

OF TIME AND SPIRIT

A Tribute to My Father

MAURICE W. DORSEY

Copyright © 2020 by Maurice W. Dorsey.

Library of Congress Control Number:		2020917439
ISBN:	Hardcover	978-1-6641-3019-7
	Softcover	978-1-6641-3020-3
	eBook	978-1-6641-3018-0

All rights reserved. No part of this book may be reproduced or transmitted in any form or by any means, electronic or mechanical, including photocopying, recording, or by any information storage and retrieval system, without permission in writing from the copyright owner.

Any people depicted in stock imagery provided by Getty Images are models, and such images are being used for illustrative purposes only. Certain stock imagery © Getty Images.

Print information available on the last page.

Rev. date: 09/18/2020

To order additional copies of this book, contact:
Xlibris
844-714-8691
www.Xlibris.com
Orders@Xlibris.com
817976

CONTENTS

Preface xiii

Introduction xvii

Chapter 1   Father Remains 1

Chapter 2   Catholic Born on Good Friday 12

Chapter 3   An Early Marriage and Children 21

Chapter 4   A Segregated United States Army 26

Chapter 5   Civilian Career Launch and Family Life 37

Chapter 6   Father Culture 61

Chapter 7   Two Plates Broken 85

Chapter 8   Breaking Plate Number 3-Mine! 104

Chapter 9   Freedom and My Dad's Discovery of Himself 122

Epilogue 147

Appendicies 149

Bibliography 161

Index 165

ALSO BY
Maurice W. Dorsey

Books

From Whence We Come

The story of an African American man who is gay and struggles to reconcile the conflict he feels between his Methodists born mother who said she never wanted to have him and a Catholic father who loved him unconditionally.

Businessman First

Remembering Henry G. Parks, Jr. (1916–1989): Capturing the Life of a Businessman Who Was African American, a Biography. More than his ad "More Parks Sausages, Mom.....Please!" was a man before his time. A historical biography tracing his journey pioneering the American free enterprise system. He embarked on a journey leading to a multi-million-dollar industry in mid-century USA.

Award

Phillis Wheatley Award Finalist, Nonfiction: *Businessman First* (Harlem Book Festival, August 30, 2015)

Articles

"Don't Forget the Founder of Parks Sausage" (*Baltimore Sun*, March 5, 2019)

"What Does Black History Mean to Me?" (*Gay City News*, February 1, 2018)

"Michael Lee-Chin" (Contributing Writer, *Black Past*, September 30, 2014)

"Henry G. Parks, Jr." (Contributing Writer, *Black Past*, September 12, 2014)

Interviews

Gay Life After 40 Spotlight (October 27, 2019)

Going North Podcast (October 11, 2018)

Cheryl Holloway's Book Blog (July 2, 2018)

University of Maryland Graduate School, Centennial Conversations (April 27, 2018)

LGBTSR (April 27, 2017)

WOCA Radio (June 24, 2017)

Vocal Expressions Blog Spot (October 12, 2015)

Baltimore Business Network Radio (June 22, 2015)

Mark McNease, Mademark Publishing (June 15, 2015)

Lou Fields, BDX Radio (August 2014)

Dr. Alvin Jones Radio (June 9, 2014)

Stu Taylor on Business (Blog Talk Radio, June 2014)

Lectures

Black Writers' Guild (Baltimore, December 1, 2018)

Reginald Lewis Museum (June 2018)

Reiter's Books (March 5, 2018)

University of Maryland Office of Graduate Diversity (February 23, 2016)

2015 Maryland Legislative Black Caucus (November 5, 2015)

DC Public Library (October 24, 2015)

Enoch Pratt Free Library (May 17, 2018 and October 21, 2015)

Baltimore Book Fair (October 26, 2015)

OutWrite LGBT Book Fair (August 1, 2015)

United States Department of Agriculture (April 2014)

Bel Air High School, Commencement Speech (June 5, 2012)

In loving memory of my father, James Roswell Dorsey Sr.

PREFACE

It is an honor for me to have lived long enough to write a historical biography of my father and his journey to inner peace. This is something he wanted to do for himself during the 1990s. He passed away before he could get this project completed. I have the privilege of documenting his life from his personal records; and I have interjected my viewpoint of his life based on my experiences with him as his youngest son.

I felt throughout my childhood and young adult years that my dad and I never connected as father and son. We communicated; however, I always thought he was remote and mentally preoccupied. As an adult, I learned that my dad was still finding himself. Our conversations were never long or in-depth. I saw him as quiet, reserved, and somewhat introverted. As a father, he was serious; and I took his words seriously. He had very little trouble out of me throughout my life. Our communication and his seriousness were not our biggest problems; he reached out to me repeatedly to engage with him and his life interest. The problem was that I was my mother's child. My mother took ownership of me, and there was only a little space for him in my childhood life. This condition, I think, had something to do with my parents' marriage more than anything I did or what my father did to me.

I was fifty-three years old when my father passed away. For many years, I never paid too much attention to my dad and the life he lived; however, he paid total attention to mine. He was twenty-eight years of age when I was born. I came along more or less seven years after my two siblings. Generational differences may have made up for much of our lack of understanding of each other. I was clearly on a different planet from my siblings. Times had changed when I was born. My parents had more

xiii

when I came along. Materially, I got more, and I was a materialistic child. Materialistic my dad was not.

When I inquired from adults about my inability to communicate with my dad, they said men of his generation did not talk much, express feelings or emotions. Their response to my inquiry applied in my case. I was a very high-feeling child. I was raised day-to-day by a very loquacious mother. She was my bedrock. I was accustomed to abundant daily conversations. Perhaps I expected this type of communication from my dad; however, we never communicated in that fashion.

As my mother tells the story, my dad wanted to have another child at the time I came along. She did not. She would tell me, "I had two children—a boy and a girl—and that is all I wanted." But since she loved my dad and he was an excellent provider, she got pregnant. Maybe my father wanted to relive the feelings of being loved by the innocence of a baby; maybe the same love he felt from his baby sister who earlier in his life passed away in a house fire, or the time that he missed with my brother and sister while he was overseas in the army. Or maybe he wanted to be discharged from the army. I don't know.

During the later years of my life, my dad told me the story of his baby sister Rosalie. He said that she adored him. My dad would describe to me vividly how his baby sister followed him around their family apartment home. She would literally grab a hold of his pant leg to get his attention as she crawled over the floor My dad felt responsible for her death. He said he loved her more than anyone in his life. His comment about loving her more than me did not reassure me because I wanted to be loved more by him. I guess I was jealous.

I remember, as a young child, running up to my dad when he returned home from work each day. I clearly remember him pushing me aside and saying, "Get down, boy!" After several attempts to gain his affection, I felt rebuffed. Maybe he wanted a baby girl instead of a boy or maybe he was having a hard time. Maybe my childhood approaches were not timely, regardless of the reason I felt rejected by my dad from a very early age; however, in retrospect I know was not.

As I look back and assess our lives, at my now age of seventy-three, I wish I could have loved him more because I have learned that he actually loved me more than I knew. He expressed his love to me in a letter when I was in my fifties. I had to learn from my life experiences with other people that my dad was the only person on earth who loved me unconditionally.

It is unfortunate that children don't have the maturity and wisdom to understand their parents at a much earlier age. If I had such maturity and wisdom, my dad and I would have had a much healthier and deeply loving relationship as father and son. After I came to the realization that my dad was totally in my corner, my self-esteem and self-confidence as an adult African American male escalated. Prior to this, my self-esteem was damaged, and I felt very insecure.

I did not come to the realization that my dad loved me unconditionally until I came out to both my parents. My dad was totally unflappable and supportive, whereas this was a feeling that I had not experienced in my journey to find myself from my birth in 1947 to the 1970s. He knew early in my life that I was born gay and allowed me to develop in my time and at my pace.

My dad diminished me and had called me stupid many times in my life. On the rare occasions in my life that I had a victory, he would tell everyone that I was "dumb and lucky." Although he loved me, there were parts of me he did not understand. His comments and slights often injured my feelings, but for the wrong reason. I endured. On the issue of my being gay, my dad's validation of me was resolute and toppled any insults that he had previously made. His understanding and support of me made all the difference to my well-being. I lived in a time and place where gays were shunned, ridiculed, and looked down upon to our faces and behind our backs. In my case, it was more so by women than men. From the moment my dad validated me, it mattered *not* what anyone else in the entire world thought of me. My dad supported me every step of the way, in coming to terms with my being gay, harder, may I add, than being African American. This was an unusual stance for most men of that era and today.

This, my third book, will be a portrait of my dad and his quest for inner peace. I received inner peace from my dad after he found his inner peace. I think that once he was content with himself, he was deeply contented with me. The story will be told from my eyes. For those who knew him very well, they will not disagree with my overall assessment of his life. As life sometimes designs it, we don't ever fully appreciate the scope and depth of our father's love until they are no longer with us. This is the case for me. I loved my dad deeply, and he loved me deeply; but there was so much more that we could have learned from each other if we could have communicated differently. His nature was introverted, calm, and quiet. My nature was extroverted, excitable, and noisy. My dad was invisible to me when I was a child and a young man. I did not see his worth. I was blinded by my youth, inexperience, and ambitions. As an adult, my dad and I conversed in many ways, and we communicated our love.

If my dad was living today, he would be over 101 years old. I feel his presence in my soul each day as I hope to rejoin him at my sunset and our new dawn. My dad and I will communicate endlessly.

As a note to the reader, I have used the words *colored*, *Negro*, *Black*, and *African American* as appropriate for the decades that I am referring to. I use the word *segregated* to refer to the Catholic Church and United States Army.

INTRODUCTION

Of Time and Spirit: A Tribute to My Father is the story of my dad and his journey to inner peace.

Further, it is a historical chronology compiled from his personal papers, military records, civilian personnel records, personal journals, notes jotted down on scraps of paper and the many conversations we had over my lifetime. Especially those conversations we had toward the end of his life when I had matured, become a man, and could glean some of his innermost feelings, thoughts, and wisdom.

My dad was fortunate to have two loving parents, a solid Catholic school education, and the love of his wife of sixty-two years, although he made horrible jokes about married life. He was the father of three college-educated children. Like many fathers, my dad was a great son, brother, husband, and father. He enlisted in the United States Army but was devastated that as a colored man, he was denied acceptance into Officer Candidate School (OCS). After serving in the military, he maintained a sterling career in the civilian world. He was active in his church and was the consummate community volunteer leader and activist. He was recognized and honored by three Maryland state governors for his service to his country, county, and community.

My dad was a very smart man and possessed many talents. He could put together and take apart almost anything. He loved challenges. He could design and build bookcases, cabinetry, and entire rooms; but he was not a trained carpenter. He wrote humorous poems about my mother. He had a great sense of humor and would tell the funniest jokes to his children. He would be heartbroken if we did not catch the punch line. I was one of those children—the last of the three children, the baby, who very often

xvii

missed the punch line; often, I found no humor in his jokes, especially if someone or a group was being ridiculed. He pointedly called me stupid.

My father enjoyed all types of music, classical to pop. He loved reading, crossword puzzles, collecting and talking about his favorite books. Over and over, he would speak of *The Razor's Edge* by W. Somerset Maugham. This book was his bible. He practically lived his life by it. He loved the book, and so did I, but for very different reasons. My dad was an athlete. He was a champion swimmer, he played golf, and he liked yoga. He could stand on his head well into his forties. He appreciated art, especially that of Paul Gauguin. He would ballroom-dance with my mother in the living room on Saturday nights on her favorite green 100-percent-wool carpet. My mother said he danced holes in her rug. He was handsome and well-groomed—that is, if he was presenting himself to the public, much less so when at home with his family, though he was presentable.

My dad had a man cave decades before it arrived on the modern scene and became fashionable. He stored his favorite libation, gin, in this cave and consumed it regularly. Gin was one of his many trademarks. There was never a question by any of his family, friends, or neighbors that gin was his drink of preference. His best friends always maintained a small stash for him whenever he visited them. This always ensured a return visit from my dad.

My dad was no chump. He tolerated almost everything, but he could be very terse, chopping you up pleasantly with his inexhaustible vocabulary when he was pushed too far. Once that happened to you, you learned to stand clear. He was never loud, nor did he use profanity. I think he learned these skills and techniques from the Catholic nuns that taught him.

He was extremely religious, but never conforming totally to biblical teachings. He always maintained his interpretation of the Bible and church laws. He questioned practices of the church and added his twist of logic if they did not make sense to him. My dad lived a life of gratitude. He was happy with the least little thing you gave him, material or otherwise. His teaching me gratitude and loving me unconditionally as a gay man were his greatest gifts to me. Most of all, my dad was a humanitarian.

For some people, his life would have been a huge achievement. My dad received esteemed recognitions to boot; however, he was seeking something more, something different. It was invisible. He did not know what it was for most of his life. As a child, I had no idea what it was either.

He always appeared odd to me—hunting, searching, and looking for the meaning of his life.

James Roswell Dorsey, Sr., was my father. He was born April 18, 1919. It was Good Friday, a revered day for Christians. With this birth date, organized religion was imprinted on his life of eighty-one years. He was born in Baltimore, Maryland, to Carrie and Leander Dorsey, who were devout in their individual practices of Christianity. Carrie was Catholic, Leander was Presbyterian. The husband and wife departed their home at the same time each Sunday morning. Carrie and her seven children attended Saint Pius Catholic Church; Leander attended the Madison Avenue Presbyterian Church.

My dad was baptized, confirmed, and given the communion in the Catholic Church. He also became an altar boy. He wrote in his notes that he was confused as a child; he prayed that his father would save himself from hell and attend the Catholic Church, whereby he would go to heaven. He wrote that he did not believe anyone could be better than a Catholic.

My dad attended Saint Pius Catholic School until eighth grade. He obtained a classical education. He developed a love of literature, classical music, and fine arts. He studied, earned good grades, and was never a conduct problem. The priest and the nuns taught being on time, and God knows, my dad was punctual for everything, and he was irritated when others were not. He believed in God and prayed he would go to heaven. As a teenager, he believed that masturbation, premarital sex, adultery, divorce, and abortion were sins.

A tragedy occurred in my dad's life that I knew nothing about until I was about forty years of age. He told me the story of how his baby sister died in a house fire. He felt responsible and carried the guilt for well over one-half of his life. I was mortified as he told me the story. He was only ten years old at the time, but somehow he felt responsible. He loved his baby sister, and he said he had never known the purity of love as he had known from his baby sister, Rosalie. The pain in his heart was unbearable to him and unbearable to me as he told me his true story. His mother said nothing to help console his sorrow and guilt. My grandmother was a good person, but stoic beyond compare from my childhood eyes. She was unmoved by my dad's inner pain and suffering. She was often described as cold. As a child, I agreed.

After eighth grade, my dad transitioned to public schools; however, his desire was to attend the St. Emma's Military Academy in Virginia.

xix

There was not enough money for both him and his older brother to attend. During that era, deference was given to the older male child, although my dad was the better student. Once in public schools, he had no problems with his studies and grades; the Catholic schools had given him a solid foundation. He gained recognition for being a champion swimmer, which earned him the school letter.

In high school he was conflicted and confused when anxious young girls pressed upon him. He knew nothing of girls. He believed a kiss before marriage was a sin. He felt guilty when he got an erection or had a wet dream. His Catholic indoctrination conflicted with his natural instincts. His solution to engaging in sexual activity was to get married.

In 1939, he married my mother. Together they had two children one year apart. At the time of their marriage, he worked at the Alcazar Social Club in Baltimore City. He worked seven days a week, earning $7 per week. He taught swimming at the YMCA part-time.

Being young and inexperienced, he didn't know that marriage would truncate the joys of singlehood or truncate his time to determine what he wanted to do with his life. He learned swiftly that he needed a more substantial job, urgently, to care for his family.

He accepted his responsibilities and, in 1941, accepted a position as a laborer at the US Army Chemical Center in Edgewood, Maryland. He took night classes at Cortez Peter's Business School to further his education but still did not know what career he wanted pursuit.

Up to this point, my dad lived in segregated housing, attended a segregated Catholic church, and was educated in segregated schools, both Catholic and public. He had never seriously experienced or was confronted with racial discrimination and racism. Segregation was all he knew.

In 1944, he enlisted in the United States Army during World War II. He was stationed in Italy, France, and Germany. He experienced for the first time in his life the harshness of discrimination and racism. All of the officers were white. My dad's service in the army was rated outstanding by his commanding officers. He was recommended for Officer Candidate School (OCS). To become an officer he thought, was a distinguished career and would be more than adequately support his family. His records were flawless; however, when they were transferred to the War Department in Washington DC, he was rejected twice. This was a body blow to his emotional spirits. His hopes of becoming an officer had been dashed. He was devastated. He then made a request to be discharged from the army based on the dependency clause. His request was granted. I, his third child, was born in May 1947.

When he returned home, he was readily accepted back to his civilian job as a laborer. His immediate supervisors thought too that he had been treated unfairly by the War Department. He was grateful to be employed, but working as a laborer was not his career aim or passion. Civilian personnel trained my dad year after year. He received promotion after promotion. By 1971, he had suffered two heart attacks and retired on disability. After working thirty-one years in federal service and earning numerous awards, he still had not found his *raison d'être*.

My dad never gave up on his dream of finding out who he was and why he was here on earth. After years of questioning Catholicism, in 1972, he joined the Ames United Methodist Church, another African American church. He found some happiness there and said he enjoyed the fellowship. He sang in the choir and was appointed as a trustee. He worked with the local chapter of the National Association for the Advancement of Colored People (NAACP). He took a basic tax class at H&R Block and was subsequently offered a part-time job; and he was the first African American to work with the Harford County Office of Property Tax Appeals. He handled the affairs of an illiterate woman for eighteen years without pay. He served in leadership positions with the American Legion, the Veterans of Foreign War (VFW), the Ruff-Ross Educational Fund, Inc., PTA and Toastmasters International. Even with his numerous engagements, he still did not find the inner peace he was seeking. He was still feeling lost; the world made no sense to him.

By a twist of fate, my sister asked my dad questions about his family genealogy for research she was conducting on our family. He suddenly became interested in finding out about himself through his family history leading to further discoveries in African American history. A friend of my sister's, Christine Tolbert, suggested my dad contact Mr. Andy Bristow, who was associated with the Harford County Historical Society, to discuss his interest in Black history. My dad asked if he could help in any way, and Mr. Bristow replied, "Come on down to the office and I will see what I can do for you."

When my dad arrived on Thursday of the following week, Mr. Bristow immediately assigned him as curator of maps. My dad struck his pot of gold. Tracing the roots of African Americans provided him with the explanations that motivated him to become the person he had become.

After working for thirty-one years in federal service and another twenty years searching for his inner contentment, my dad found his passion in African American history at the Harford County Historical Society.

During the 1990s, my dad purchased a personal computer with every intention of documenting the footprints of his life. He was anxious and ecstatic setting up and connecting each of the components of his computer and mobilizing his thoughts to paper. He was a lover of the new technology, gadgets, and attempts to look into the future. He even liked *Star Trek* for an example and watched it religiously. I thought my dad was weird, and I thought the program was weird too. Needless to say, my dad and I did not agree or synchronize on many issues, but we accepted and loved each other unconditionally. There was nothing he would not do for me. When I was a young child, he often called my behaviors stupid disapproved of me for not loving what he loved. I thought his behaviors were stupid too, but neither of us budged on our respective positions. We peacefully kept it moving, as the young folk say today.

Upon his death in December 2000, I inherited all the papers from my dad's man cave. My mother was eighty years old at the time and said to me, "Just take all that junk out of here!" I did not want to discard the papers that he spent a lifetime collecting. I was fifty-three years old, and my career had finally accelerated. However, I could not discard something that was so tremendously important to him. I knew he had purchased a computer for the sole purpose of writing his book, and he never got the chance to write it due to poor health and age. He waited too long to start writing and may have been confused and overwhelmed as to where to start, as I am. I have held these papers for almost twenty years and now have finally organized my dad's life in this book—*Of Time and Spirit*—in a way that I think he would appreciate. He would smile to see that his life is recorded somewhere in history as he had always dreamed. I know it falls short of his high intellect, but it is an accurate stab at his life through my eyes.

It is my hope that by publishing this book, I can help fathers around the world can see the importance of their lives to their children. My dad's life, although I often misunderstood it as a child, was a clear gift to me as an adult.

My dad passed away on December 2, 2000. This is where my story begins. The ascension of a child born on Good Friday.

CHRONOLOGY

Born April 18, 1919, on Good Friday.

Graduated Saint Pius Primary School, 1933.

Graduated Frederick Douglass Junior High School, 1934.

Athletic Certificate, Frederick Douglass High School, 1936.

Graduated Frederick Douglass High School, Academic, 1937.

Married Zelma Virginia Curry, 1939.

First child born, 1940.

Second child born, 1941.

Employed by the Army Chemical Center, Edgewood Arsenal, Maryland, 1941.

Order to Report for Induction, United States Army, 1944.

Honorable Discharge, United States Army, 1946.

Third child born, 1947.

Certificate, Fundamentals of Electronics, De Forest's Training, Inc., Chicago, Illinois, 1951.

Diploma, Radio Television and Servicing, De Forest's Training, Inc., Chicago, Illinois, 1952.

Training Course, Principles and Maintenance of Foxboro Instruments, Foxboro, Massachusetts, 1953.

Beckman Instruments Training, Fullerton, California, 1954.

Taylor Instruments Training, Rochester, New York, 1955.

Training Course, Principles and Maintenance of Foxboro Instruments, Foxboro, Massachusetts, 1957.

Certificate, Instrument Training Course, the Bristol Company, Waterbury, Connecticut, 1959.

Home ownership, 1960.

Certificate of 20 Years of Federal Service, Department of the Army, 1961.

Certificate, Introduction to Supervision, Department of the Army, 1962.

Certificate, Supervisors Safety Training, Department of the Army, 1963.

Course, Dekatron Machine Theory and Maintenance, Sciaky Brothers, Inc., Chicago, Illinois, 1963.

Certificate, Theory of Operation, Calibration, and Maintenance, CoHu Electronics Training, San Diego, California, 1964.

Certificate, Effective Writing, Department of the Army, 1967.

Officially commended and cash award, United States Army, 1968.

Course, Industrial Instrumentation, Honeywell, Inc., Fort Washington, Pennsylvania, 1969.

Certificate, Chemical Biological Surety Program Course for Supervisors, Department of the Army, 1970.

Certificate of 30 Years of Federal Service, United States Army, 1971.

Certificate of Retirement, Department of the Army, 1972.

Harford County Property Tax Assessment Appeal Board, 1978–1988.

Black History Publication: "Religion: Convictions Run Deep," 1995.

Governor's Citation, Parris N. Glendening, October 1996.

Harford County Historic Preservationist Award, 2000.

CHAPTER 1

Father Remains

2000

Wednesday, December 6, 2000, was the day of my dad's funeral. I gently walked into the Ames United Methodist Church in Bel Air, Maryland, with my mother firmly holding on to my arm. Her arm felt like a skintight clutch to my lean arm. It was a sad day for her and a sad day for me. I knew that I had to be strong for her, and, from within, I thought for me too. It would have been what my dad wanted. He was one of the trustees of the church. Ames was the first African American church in Bel Air.

It was a cold and clear December day, and the sun was shining bright. The grounds of the church were manicured, and the air was thin and fresh, which made the entry into the church easier; and I really felt that my air passages were open and ready to breathe during this celebration of my dad's life.

My mother and I were followed by my brother and his wife, then my sister and her husband. Other family members followed. I could see and feel the light, the colors, and the cleanliness of the church interior. Although this church is located in a rather rural county in Maryland, it was as majestic as an Italian cathedral. The sanctuary was warm and colorful as the sunlight shone through the stained glassed windows. The church was simple and tastefully fashioned. The front of the church was adorned with fresh flowers from family and friends, flanking the sides of my dad's casket.

1

My parents had purchased their grave plots, their grave liners and markers for their burial many years prior to the funeral. My mother and I selected the casket from the McComas Family Funeral Homes. We ordered two dozen red roses from Richardson Florist to place atop the open half of the casket. My dad was a man who saw the beauty in almost any variety flower; and had he been living, he would have enjoyed the view that I had on this day. He was flawlessly dressed and groomed. I purchased a new white shirt for him and used one of his many church suits for the services.

My dad's extended family, friends, and associates were all seated as our immediate family entered the sanctuary from the waiting area. It appeared that every seat in the church was occupied. I wanted to snap with emotions because the pressure was unbearable as the time was nearing. When I look back, I wonder if perhaps it was my mother holding me up versus me holding her for she knew me and how emotional I was as a man.

The people who were gathered were well-dressed, dignified, and stately as they awaited the services to commence. There were town officials and community and neighborhood leaders in attendance. I could see as we enter the church the crowns of African American women. They were positioned on their heads to perfection. Although it was winter, the assortment of hats appeared like a spring garden as I looked on. The brims on some of the hats were so large they appeared to be taking up space for two seats.

After being seated, my mother disengaged her arm from mine. I was relieved to be released, I could feel the perspiration accumulating under my arm and wrinkling of my sleeves. I sat very silent, upright, anxious, and somewhat petrified as to what was going to happen next. The preparation and coordination of a funeral is a lot of work, and on the day of the service, you are simply exhausted from the hectic planning and turnarounds. This was my first experience with the death of a parent. And let me tell the readers that if you have never experienced the death of a parent, it is like a feeling you have never felt before in your entire life. And if you loved your parent deeply, it is much worse.

After all the congregation and the church clergy were seated, my mind rambled down the path of my dad's life as I anticipated the commencement of the funeral. My mind regressed to stories of my dad's boyhood, his Catholic schooling, his military experiences, his career struggles, his achievements, and his lifetime pursuit of inner peace. My mind also concentrated on our lifelong struggles to communicate as father and son.

Of Time and Spirit

While reflecting, I felt surrounded by the love of those lives he touched, and who also cared enough to pay their final respects to a respectable man.

My dad had suffered two heart attacks earlier in his life. His first heart attack occurred at about age forty-eight, the second at about the age fifty-three. When my mother called to inform me of the first attack, I was in undergraduate school at the University of Maryland, College Park. I remained calm for her. At that time, I was learning to be an adult. My mother could be highly emotional, but this time, she sounded weary but was performing her wifely and motherly duties. I was young and did not know much about human health or the process of getting older. I remember my dad as tall, handsome, and physically fit man. It was hard at the time to conceptualize a heart attack other than to know it was serious health ailment.

I guess, I selectively remembered the years when he would to do sit-ups and push-ups and balance himself on his head on the living room carpet. He was a champion swimmer, and he played golf. The heart attack did not fit my vision of my dad. I did ask my mother when she called me if he was still alive, and she said yes, and I felt relief for me and for her; but it was a dreamlike image for me. It was difficult to imagine my father being sick at all.

It was a miserable feeling not being at home and not knowing just what to say to my mother. My emotions and all sorts of feelings emerged. My mother told me not to come home because there was nothing I could do, but the conflict inside my soul wanted me to be there, and at the same time, I wanted to honor her request of not creating more stress for her. "You stick with your studies," she said.

I had somehow forgotten that my dad loved high-salt and high-cholesterol food, like eggs, bacon, butter, whole milk, steak, beef kidney stew, Longhorn cheese, saltines, kosher dill pickles, and half and half in his coffee. He said he quit smoking at the age of thirty-five, but he continued to drink gin his entire life before and after his heart attacks. Gin was my dad's trademark libation. If anybody knew him well, they knew he liked gin. My mother said he was drinking gin miniatures when she met him. If I had remembered all these things, I should have known a second heart attack was inevitable.

When he later had a second heart attack, his doctors stated that he needed to have quadruple bypass heart surgery. He clearly stated before my mother and me in the living room at home that he did not want to have

3

the surgery. My dad had never been in a hospital a day in his life before his heart attacks. He hated doctors and the prescriptions they recommended. He thought too that prescription drugs went against the body's natural rhythm, and he sought homeopathic methods to treat himself. I don't know what he thought his consumption of gin did to his natural rhythm.

At this point in my life, I was the child who felt least close to my dad because we had little in common, probably because I was terribly close to my mother. I looked at my dad and said, "Dad, you must have the surgery!" I said it as a matter of fact. I was absolute but gentle with my statement. I am sure he was wondering under what authority I could make such a statement, considering we were not soulmates at that time, and he was the father and in charge of his life.

My dad looked me in the face and said, "Why?"

I really didn't know why, but I replied, "Because you have not finished raising me. You still have more work to do with me!"

It was a silly statement since I was a grown man, a homeowner, a college graduate with two graduate degrees. What more could he have done? I must have been in some type of denial mode that I could not explain. I knew for sure I was not ready for him to die; I wanted to give him a reason to keep living.

My dad dejectedly, and without equivocation, said, "All right, then!"

I believe my dad underwent quadruple bypass surgery, for me. I would suspect it made him feel needed, loved, and important to someone. It was amazing to me that he did not seem to feel any more loved than me at that time.

I was a young adult at this point, but we both knew that he and I had not completed our parent-child cycle, whatever that was. In any event, I was clearly not ready for him to die, yet our reason for being in each other's life was not clear to me either. He was my father and the provider for our family. He was quiet and introspective—a thinking, writing, and performance-and-achievement type of man.

My dad arrived at the Johns Hopkins University Hospital for the second time, and after he was prepped for the surgery, the doctors quietly warned my mother that this was a serious surgery and that my dad may not make it through the procedures. I guess he wanted us to be prepared. My mother and I braced ourselves with the doctor's warning, squeezing each other's hand just as tight as we had at this funeral. We walked with the doctors and nurses by the gurney that held my dad's body. There were hoses, cords, pipes, needles in my dad's arms; his head was wrapped, and he was covered with those sanitary cotton blankets. It was like a scene from the movie *One Flew Over the Cuckoo's Nest.*

My mother held my dad's hands, nervously repeating, "Everything will be all right," as the orderlies were almost running down the hospital halls, on highly polished floors and sanitary white walls, until we approached the double swing doors and were no longer permitted beyond them. The signage announced Hospital Staff Only. This was the moment that the surgery was going to be performed. I don't know why, but I knew he was going to be OK as I pulled my mother away from the doors as they closed in our faces, giving me a true sense of finality. The surgery was going to be done.

I hated to see my mother cry anytime; but on this occasion, I knew she was scared, saying out loud to the doctors and nurses who pushed the gurney, "My husband has never spent a day in the hospital his whole life." She knew he was afraid. He said, he didn't want the surgery in the first place. She knew he did not like doctors. Tears fell from her eyes uncontrollably as the automatic swing doors shut.

My dad was knocked out by the time he entered the operating room. I remained calm for my mother. We waited for eight hours. When the doctor returned to the waiting room, he informed my mother that the surgery was a success. At that moment, I cried from the release of pressure I had held from the waiting and the anticipation of the outcome. My dad made it through the surgery. He was going to live, just as I had expected and needed him to do. I had no idea why I needed him to live against his wishes. He was always a self-sacrificing man and, subconsciously, to me too. He always gave me what I asked for, always.

At the time of his surgery, I lived in Baltimore County, Maryland. I worked in Washington DC, and it was a hundred-mile round-trip drive for me. I commuted each day from home to the Johns Hopkins University Hospital in Baltimore City before starting work at 8:30 AM in Washington DC. I would return to the hospital after work, then return home. It was a long stretch—five hours a day commuting back and forth through the Baltimore Harbor Tunnel to the Baltimore-Washington Parkway to Interstate 695, a.k.a. Capital Beltway. I was feeling purposeful; I had meaning for the first time in my life. My dad was important, and I got my chance to take care of him. I had no children and was excited about caring for him.

I was dressed in a suit and tie each time I entered the hospital after his surgery. I kindly requested that the doctors, nurses, the receptionist, and anybody I saw to please take care of my dad. Hospitals use to be segregated. However, after the integration, Negros in white hospitals were not treated well unless someone was standing guard and looking respectable. I was standing guard for my dad. My mother was getting old, fatigued, and had her health issues. However, I stepped in and took over for her just as she would have done had she been younger, rested, and in better health. She gave me orders like she was the Queen of England, and I performed each and every one. I was relentless in making sure somebody was caring for my father each day, both morning and night. By this time, I had learned the word "gratitude"—a word my dad taught me. I was feeling grateful for him just breathing. It is an out-of-mind-and-body experience.

After entering the workforce and gaining my independence, I knew how hard it was for an African American man to get a job, keep a job, and hope for overdue, deserved promotions. My dad suffered through all of this for a wife and three children for thirty years. I knew it was hard for him because my career experiences were not too far afield without wife or children. He had a hard time; he was not highborn, and neither was I.

When my dad was discharged from the hospital, I helped my mother take care of him. I felt as though he was my child. I was grateful for him, and it was my honor, duty, and joy to repay the good he had done for me throughout my life, much of which I was too young to appreciate. I only knew that he had never wronged me deliberately.

My dad retired from Edgewood Arsenal after this second heart attack. Medical health care had improved in the five years that followed his first attack. The doctors said this time he was as good as new, but he chose to retire anyway. For an African American man in the federal government, he was earning great money and could have earned more. Times were changing, and civil rights laws were beginning to be enforced. But my dad was never money driven, never greedy or materialistic. He elected a disability and retired with thirty-one years of service at age fifty-three. He thrived for many years afterward.

Before his retirement, he liked to play the Maryland Lottery. After retirement, he upgraded his gambling habit to the slot machines in Atlantic City, New Jersey, and Delaware Park. In an effort to give my mother a break from the care and routines of caring for herself and my dad, I drove Dad to Delaware Park to play the slot machines one Saturday early afternoon. The incisions from his surgery were still rather raw He was always excited to get out of the house and to play the slots. He won and lost, both in the thousands of dollars. He had earned and saved enough discretionary money that he could splurge on the slot machines several times a year. Although you will read later that my dad had a very active and productive life, at this point, his interest in life had become minimal.

While we were driving along Interstate 95 North, I said, "Dad, I know you did not think I was paying attention to you as a child, but I have something I want to play for you." I inserted a CD in the CD player of my car, and out bellowed the *Overture to Tannhauser* by Richard Wagner, Barry Wordsworth, Conductor, New Queens Hall Orchestra in all of its musical splendor. At its commencement the orchestra rehearses the song of pilgrims, which, as it approaches, grows louder and louder and, at length, recedes. This was my dad's favorite of all classical music selections. He had played it for me for the first time when I was ten years old. I learned to love it too.

When my dad heard the very familiar music, he got so emotional he cried. He cried so hard his nose started to run, and he pulled out his white starched and hand-ironed handkerchief to dry his eyes and to wipe his runny nose. I was astonished, for I had never, in forty years, seen my dad show emotion over anything—never, not for anything. I thought I was going to have to pull the car over to console him. He settled his emotions, and we continued to proceed to the slot machines in Delaware Park. He was speechless for a period, and the conversation was dry as the music played on. He eventually said, "Thank you, son!"

What makes *Tannhauser* such a divine piece of music is that it releases, through orchestration, the listener from ungodliness when two divided elements—spirit and mind, God and nature—embrace each other in the holy uniting Kiss of Love. Needless to say, my dad was touched by what I had done to make him feel like a good father and teacher. This was an honor I had not expressed to him for many years prior.

Afterwards, I played the CD from the musical *La Cage aux Follies*. *La Cage* opened on Broadway in 1983. It broke barriers for gays by becoming one of the first hit Broadway musicals centered on a homosexual relationship. The shows one-act finale brought fullness to my gay life whenever the musical selection "I Am What I Am" played. The original production ran for more than four years and won six Tony Awards. The book was written by Harvey Forbes Fierstein—actor, playwright, singer, and voice actor.

I was going to introduce my dad to a piece of music I had come to like as a gay man. He was astonished. As worldly and cultured as my dad was, he had never heard *La Cage aux Follies*. The contrast between *La Cage aux Follies* and the *Prelude to Tannhauser* was a painful example of the difference between my dad and me. I continued to play the music, but he seemed afraid of the lyrics. The music I played for him on this day was as different as night and day.

Unfortunately, almost every conversation we had with each other throughout our lives was painfully excruciating. Yet this was my dad who loved me unconditionally. Parents live through each stage of their child's development sometimes with fear and questioning of what is going on inside their child's brain. This was one of those moments. Whatever the psychological explanation, the feelings between us remained mutual. I loved my dad unconditionally.

After we arrived at the casino, I placed $200 in my dad's hand, knowing that he had his own money. I was showing off my success. He accepted the money and said enthusiastically and with mild disbelief, "Hey, Jughead! Thanks!"

I said, "If you win big, are you going to share your winnings with me?"

He laughed and said, "No, siree!" However, from knowing my dad as I did, he would have given me all of his winnings if I wanted it. For some reason, we were two complicated men, but we struggled like drowning swimmers trying to save each other's lives, for the purpose of just demanding to understand each other.

When my dad and I arrived at the casino, we synchronized our watches and agreed to meet at the foot of the first-floor escalators in two hours. Of course, I had no interest in being in a casino or losing my money, so I simply had lunch and read the Broadway reviews in the *New York Times* and waited while he enjoyed his time away from home.

When the two hours had expired, I waited for my father to meet me at the foot of the escalators. After ten, fifteen, twenty, and thirty minutes had lapsed, I began to get warm. I got a little sweaty, but I did not want to move from the designated spot thinking he would show up while I went to look for him. My dad was a stickler for time, and he was always punctual and never late for anything. As I was preparing to go to the information desk to page my dad, I saw him descending the escalator. He looked at me with glee and said, "Maurice? What are you doing up here?"

What? I thought. I looked at him and said as lovingly as I could, "I brought you to the casino today, Daddy!" My heart plunged. It was one of the most awkward moments in my life with my father, the reversal of roles, with me needing to take care of him versus him taking care of me. He was suffering from the beginning of dementia.

After both heart attacks, my dad tired of taking his medications and substituted gin for medications. He was in bad shape. He was in and out of the hospital, and I helped my mother in every way possible until eventually, they sold the family house that they had lived in for forty years and moved to a very nice apartment in Owings Mills, Maryland. I was happy to show affection and love for him. I had curtains custom-made for his bedroom and purchased a new desk for him. He loved organizing his papers and files. My mother organized his bed and wardrobe. He would settle in almost anywhere you put him, and he was happy not to be worried with cutting grass and maintaining the old house. An apartment was all he ever wanted in the first place. He never wanted homeownership; this was my mother's idea, and it was a grand idea because the proceeds from the sale of the house had huge returns, for the land value more so than the house value.

He eventually became too much for my mother to handle, and her health was deteriorating. She and I drove around the city looking for nursing homes, one after the other, to the extent of pure exhaustion. I was still commuting between Baltimore and Washington DC to take care of business. My mother settled on the nicest veterans' hospital in the city by way of a high school contact of my sister's. My mother refused to place him in some of the dreadful places we had visited. For me, seeing some senior citizen accommodation early in life lets you know that old age is hell, and doubly worse if you have no money. My mother had visited the elderly in old folks' homes and learned this lesson many years earlier in her life.

I visited my dad at the Loch Raven VA Medical Center on Loch Raven Boulevard. Each time I visited, I would help him to his wheelchair and push him through the halls of the hospital if it were damp or rainy or follow the walking path outside on the property. On one occasion, we approached a rather steep elevation on the walking path, and he could see the cars through the trees moving in both directions of the median strip on Loch Raven Boulevard. He said to me: "You know, Maurice, you could just take this wheelchair and push me over the cliff." His comment really, really broke my heart. He could not see me from behind as I pushed his wheelchair, but I cried at the thought of his statement. What had happened to the dad I knew? I could feel my dad slipping away from me, and it was massively unnerving for me. Psychologically, I got very fatigued as if I were going to faint.

When I returned him to his hospital bed, he thanked me for taking him to get some fresh air and for purchasing his favorite candy bar: Mr. Goodbar. He sat on the side of his bed looking very handsome, considering he was so sick inside his mind and body. He said to me, "Maurice, my life is over."

As much as I talked, I could not find the words to answer, but my best effort was to smile gently and say, "Well, Dad, you did an outstanding job raising me." In my heart, I thought he had been holding on to his life because I asked him to do so, for my benefit. I didn't think he wanted to hurt me with his dying. How unselfish on his part. It was time for me to let him go. He had suffered long enough. I felt dreadful, deep down dreadful. I still feel dreadful when I recall him saying this to me.

When I reached the Baltimore-Washington Parkway to return home, I prayed that God would take my dad. He had suffered long enough. He had given me all he had to give. I don't know if God heard my prayer or if it was just my dad's time; but three days later, on December 2, the family was called together, and my dad took his last breath, with his wife and three children at his side. It is a feeling like nothing I had ever felt before. I lost a parent, role model, and dearest friend. My dad's death was so final that I could not cry at that moment, but once the tears started, I have been periodically crying since then.

My dad was a lover of English poet, playwright, and actor William Shakespeare. Shakespeare is regarded as the greatest writer in the English language. My dad loved his poem "The Seven Ages of Man." The last two words of the poem are "sans everything." This day was my dad's "sans everything."

My mother's emotional burst of tears caused by a pronouncement by Reverend Eric W. King, Sr., who delivered the eulogy, awakened me from my reflections on my dad's final days. When I returned to reality, I turned around to see if my drawn-out mental absence was noticed. As I inched my head around discreetly to look, I could see there was not a dry eye in the church. I turned my head back toward the casket, then looked at the

Of Time and Spirit

program. I had neglected much of the singing, prayers, acknowledgments, and readings from the Old and New Testaments of the Bible; but I was at peace with my dad. My prayer was answered. We then traveled to the gravesite by way of limousine. A few prayers were said, and then the ceremony was over, and my dad was laid to rest. He was eighty-one years old.

My dad said to me in front of my mother before his death, "Maurice, I want you to see to it that I get a decent burial." And it was magnificent, if a funeral is ever magnificent. As for me, my father remains.

CHAPTER 2

Catholic Born on Good Friday

1919

My dad was born at home on April 18, 1919, 4:00 a.m. This was on a Good Friday, a highly religious day for Christians. It is a Christian holiday commemorating the crucifixion of Jesus and his death at Calvary. It is observed during Holy Week on the Friday preceding Easter Sunday and sometimes coincides with the Jewish observance of Passover. Although it was celebrated differently all over the world, my dad's family honored all the traditions of the Catholic Church: fasting, church services, stations of the cross, and novenas to the Divine Mercy. There was no dancing or horsing around on this day. My grandmother would purchase hot cross buns during Holy Week every year. As a child I looked forward to the treat with a juice glass of orange juice.

My dad was also born ten years before the crash of the New York Stock Exchange on October 23, 1929. It was the most devastating stock market crash in the history of the United States. This was the signal of the Great Depression. These were difficult times for my dad's family considering they were a colored family of no social importance but to themselves. My dad's family was not highborn or of wealth, excesses, or privilege.

My dad's family lived at 623 Pitcher Street, Baltimore, Maryland, Ward 14, when he was born. The attending doctor was Bernard Hughes of 1413 Druid Hill Avenue. My dad's father was Leander Edward Dorsey, and

12

Of Time and Spirit

his mother was Carrie Elizabeth Snowden-Dorsey. They were respectable colors and benefited from a high fair complexion.

My dad's father was a janitor and elevator operator. He was promoted over the years to storeroom manager. As a child, I thought he was a tailor because he worked at Hass Tailoring located on Sinclair Lane off Erdman Avenue in East Baltimore. Hass Tailoring was in business for over one hundred years. The client list for this company included Bill Clinton, Bob Dole, George Bush, Arsenio Hall, James Earl Jones, and Colin Powell. Hass Tailoring outlasted seventy-five-year-old London Fog Industries, also a Baltimore manufacturing plant.

My grandfather wore tailor-made suits to church every Sunday. For a colored man of his generation and socioeconomic level, wearing a tailor-made suit made him the talk of the town. His wardrobe was full of fine-tailored suits.

My grandfather was well loved at Hass Tailoring. They made him a new suit every year for a bonus. My grandfather was of very fair complexion, muscular, and bald with an oversized nose. My grandfather had throat cancer and lost his speech. He had a tracheostomy. The hole in his neck was frightful to me as a child. The hole served as an airway for him to breathe without the use of his nose or mouth. I could understand his sounds and would ask him questions. He chewed on a Dutch Masters cigar and drank Christian Brothers wine. He looked to me like a wealthy white man. My dad's mother was a housewife. She too was of very fair complexion, elegant, and slightly taller than her husband. She looked white to me as well. My dad was the second child in Leander and Carrie's marriage.

My dad was born to two devout Christian parents. His mother was Catholic and his father Presbyterian. My dad was steeped in and imprinted with religious teachings and morality codes at birth.

According to Catholic Church law, when a Catholic married a non-Catholic, all the children of the marriage were required to be raised Catholic. After my father and his older brother Edward were born, Leander and Carrie had six additional siblings. My dad said one child was stillborn, one died in a house fire. As the oldest child, Edward was lovingly called the Chief.

All my father's brothers and sisters were baptized and confirmed by a Catholic priest. They were educated in segregated Catholic schools. They were taught by the Oblate Sisters of Providence, an all-black order of nuns.

13

My dad's grandfather was white, and all his children were light complexed and born free. When Leander married Carrie, although of very fair complexion, some of their children were light and some were brown. The brown color gene came from the Snowden side of our family, my grandmother. My dad had a complex about his brown complexion because he said his grandmother Dorsey discriminated against him. As an adult, I told him he was crazy because I was the same color as him and I loved my coloring. Plus, my dad was good-looking, actually better looking than his parents or any of his siblings, in my opinion.

Both of my dad's parents maintained their birth religions throughout their marriage of over fifty years. In my dad's notes, and as told in family stories too, my grandmother and my grandfather walked out of the front door of their home every Sunday morning, Carrie and the children turned to the right going to St. Barnabas Catholic Church on Biddle Street between Argyle and Pennsylvania Avenues. His father turned left and went to the Madison Avenue Presbyterian Church. None of the family missed Sunday church unless the circumstances were extremely dire. To miss mass on Sunday in the Catholic Church was a sin. If you were unable to get to confession, to confess all your sins before you died, you went straight to hell. This was Catholic Church law; this is what was taught in Catholic school. It was strict and ineradicable. My dad believed this church law even as a young child; it was preposterous to me, but children were seen and not heard, thus I knew to keep my thoughts to myself.

My dad wrote in his notes that he thought his father was a good man, but he had difficulty understanding why his dad would not leave the Presbyterian Church. "How could a Presbyterian be as nice as a Catholic?" he wrote. He prayed that his dad would become a Catholic, "to save himself from hell."

Catholic Church indoctrination was deeply instilled and ingrained in my dad. He acknowledged that his dad worked hard. He wrote that his family did not have much. He thought everybody lived the way he did. He was taught in the Catholic Church that life on earth was temporary, and your job on earth was to save your soul, for all will die. He believed and was certain there was a heaven, and he was working toward going there. My dad was an obedient Catholic.

As an adult, I never heard him speak of the house on Pitcher Street where he was born, or Stricker Street where his family once resided. He always talked about the apartment building where he lived on 1028 Eutaw

Street, home of the Maryland State Office Building. This to me always sounded like his home. My dad told stories of how he, as a child, washed the steps from the first floor down to the front steps. He shoveled ashes from the coal stove that heated the house and placed then in a tin can.

I recall when the Maryland Lottery came into existence, he and his sister played their childhood house number: 1028. Sometimes they hit, and other times he missed it by a day or two, or by a digit or two. Either way, it brought some joy to celebrate his home address. He said that during the Great Depression, Christmas would sometimes be a tangerine and a pair of gloves for each child. Everyone was grateful.

He wrote in his journal,

> I lived at 1028 North Eutaw Street during prohibition. I would gather ½ pint whiskey bottles from the back allies and sell them for 2 cents each to a man on Preston Street called Mr. Bob. He lived in a basement on Preston Street between Eutaw and Madison Avenue across from The Try Me Bottling Company.

> Located at 1030 North Eutaw Street. On the third floor, there lived a man who shall remain nameless, who got white alcohol in five-gallon tin cans. He put it in the bathtub and diluted it with water. He had me burn sugar in a pan until it was dark brown. He then placed some of the alcohol in a big crock and added the burnt sugar that was whisky. The uncolored white alcohol was gin. This man, his wife, and one child were the best dressed in the block.

I would guess this was around the time my dad started drinking gin. The consumption of alcohol and gambling were permissible in the Catholic Church, but the use of birth control was forbidden. What a combination. There were alcoholics from the Catholic Snowden side of our family.

My dad told stories of his attendance at St. Pius Catholic School on Fremont Avenue, where he graduated eighth grade in June 1933. Catholic schools were segregated. In my generation, I could not imagine a church as being segregated. This made no sense to me. However, my dad received a solid classical education from the nuns. He said my grandfather would have all the children sit around the radio at home; they listened to classical music and world events. My dad was the most classically oriented man I have ever known. He shared his father's practice of exposing his children to all of his teachings, with the exception of Catholicism.

My dad was a reader and a scholar at a young age. He was bullied and ridiculed in school by his classmates because his older brother, the Chief, was a behavior problem in class. Young boys being mischievous was considered more boyish, a good thing, and their rite of passage to manhood. The nuns compared the two brothers. The nuns would chastise the Chief, remarking, "Now, Edward, why can't you be like your brother James." My dad would recoil. The male students teased my dad: "Now, James, why can't you be like your brother Edward?"

My dad did not like being compared to his brother, nor did he like the backlash from his peers. He wanted to be included with the boys. My dad was ridiculed for being well behaved and smart. Being accepted by his peers was important, but it necessitated his being more mischievous and less studious.

While at Saint Pius, my dad studied and fell in love with the works of William Shakespeare (1564–1616). He memorized Shakespeare's works. He recited Shakespeare to my brother, sister, and me just like an English professor, or perhaps as the nuns read it to him in school. He thought it was a life lesson that he wanted all his children to grasp. My dad wanted my mother to pay attention too.

One of his favorites was Macbeth, *As You Like It*, Act II, Scene 7, Line 139.

All the world's a stage,
And all the men and women merely players.
They have their exits and their entrances;
And one man in his time plays many parts,
His acts being seven ages. At first the infant,
Mewling and puking in the nurse's arms.
And then the whining school-boy, with his satchel
And shining morning face, creeping like snail
Unwilling to school. And then the lover,
Sighing like furnace, with a woeful ballad
Made to his mistress' eyebrow. Then a Soldier,
Full of strange oaths, and bearded like the pard;

Jealous in honour, sudden and quick in quarrel,
Seeking the bubble reputation
Even in the cannon's mouth. And then the justice,
In fair round belly with good capon lin'd,
With eyes severe and beard of formal cut,
Full of wise saws and modern instances;
And so, he plays his part. The sixth age shifts
Into the lean and slipper'd pantaloons,
With spectacles on nose and pouch on side:
His youthful hose, well sav'd
a world too wide
For is shrunk shank; and his big manly voice,
Tuning again toward childish treble, pipes
And whistles in the sound. Last scene of all.
That ends his strange eventful history,
Is second childishness, and mere oblivion?
Sans teeth, sand eyes, sans taste, sans everything.

My dad also recited to us Act V, Scene 5, Lines 17–28 from *Macbeth*.

To-morrow, and to-morrow,
Creeps in this petty pace from day to day,
To the last syllable of recorded time;
And all our yesterdays have lighted fools
The way to dusty death. Out, Out brief candle!
Life's but a walking shadow, a poor player
That struts and frets his hour upon the stage
And is heard no more: it is a tale
Told by an idiot, full of sound and fury,
Signifying nothing.

My dad recited these poems and others throughout his life as a testament to his belief in their truth: *Life is a stage, and it signifies nothing.*

When schools were closed for the summer months, my dad and his older brother, the Chief, would travel to Bowie, Maryland. This is where their mother, Carrie, was raised. It was a farm. They would board trains at Pennsylvania Station. Presenting their tickets to a uniformed conductor. The conductors were white; the cars weren't segregated that he recalled.

17

The young boys were instructed to be alert when the conductors entered the car and shouted, for there was no public address system. Next stop Laurel, Maryland, because the next stop was Bowie. They were to disembark the train at the Bowie station.

My dad wrote that his step-grandad would be waiting in a buggy. There was one small suitcase for the two boys. Luggage was not a problem. After they settled in the buggy and began their journey to the farm, they were surprised by the distance they had to travel to reach their destination. While they bounced along in the buggy seats, they were awed by the trees and the purity of the fresh country air compared to that of the city. He wrote that after arriving at the farm, he would drink milk directly from the cow.

My dad recalled that after schools had closed for the day he played under a wooden bridge on Biddle and Argyle Streets. He often referred to walking up Hoffman Street as a good memory. He was happy and content during those years of his youth. As he approached his teen years, he took great interest in being well-groomed and neatly dressed. He was a refined young man, of good character, and possessed great deportment.

After completing eighth grade in the Catholic school setting, his parents transitioned him to public schools, whereby they could afford to send the younger children to Catholic schools. He attended Frederick Douglass Junior High School in Baltimore. The transition was very different. The students were more liberated and expressed themselves when it was uninvited. He was not accustomed to having a voice in Catholic school. You spoke when spoken to and did what you were told. My dad tried to raise his children this way, but the times had changed, and we did not attend Catholic schools.

My dad was not accustomed to the noise in the classrooms and hallways, nor to the aggressiveness of the students. The classes were larger, and the teachers were not uniformly dressed, as were the nuns in Catholic school. The girls took a strong liking to him. He managed, however, to maintain his Catholic disciplines and to succeed academically.

He became a competitive swimming champion and received an athletic certificate and school letter for swimming on May 29, 1936. My dad had mastered the techniques of swimming in such detail that he was utilized as a student-teacher. He taught basic swimming after school to students who were having difficulties in mastering swimming skills. Harry T. Pratt was the school principal, and Alan A. Watty was the school coach.

After Catholic school, my dad had a strong desire to attend St. Emma's Military Academy, a Catholic private school, in Powhatan, Virginia. Becoming an officer in the military was just about as high up in the career food chain as a colored man could expect to attain. Even as a youngster, he stated that he wanted to become a soldier. He had two uncles who served in the military—one in the army and the other in the navy during World War II. He said he loved to listen to them tell stories, and he was proud of their pictures in their uniforms.

St. Emma's Military Academy was an all-black, all-male Catholic military school. It was an industrial and agricultural institute. It was once a premier school. As an in-state agricultural school, St. Emma was second only to Virginia Polytechnic Institute, Blacksburg. It was built on a former plantation that once housed slaves. In 2004, the Sisters of the Blessed Sacrament, an order of Catholic women who owned the Belmead property, formed the 501c(3) nonprofit corporation FrancisEmma, Inc., to preserve the land and develop educational programs.

These were hard times for colored people before, during, and after the Great Depression of 1929. There was not enough money in the family for the Chief and my dad to attend St. Emma's. The Chief, the oldest son, was heir to the privilege. This was a missed opportunity for my dad. Due to his position in the birth order and the cultural mores of the time. The first son was always heir to first opportunities. My dad understood the pecking order of things but saw himself as the more serious student. He felt he should have had this opportunity more than his older brother, who had a behavior problem and less serious about his studies. My dad held hurt feelings for years over this injustice. However the Chief did not complete this program and my dad thought it was a complete waste of money and this aggravated his sensitivity. The Chief sent his only son, Michael, to St. Emma's, and he did complete the program. This was an age-old family drama!

My dad graduated junior and senior high school from Frederick Douglass High School. He earned an academic diploma on June 21, 1937. Harry T. Pratt was the principal, Forrest Bramble was president of the school commission and David E. Weglein was the superintendent of public instruction. Frederick Douglass was originally named the Colored High and Training School. Douglass was the second oldest high school created specifically for African American students in Baltimore. Prior to desegregation, Douglass and Paul Laurence Dunbar High Schools were the only two high schools that admitted African American students, with Douglass serving West Baltimore and Dunbar serving students in East Baltimore. Former Supreme Court justice Thurgood Marshall is one of Douglass's most notable alumni.

Although attending St. Emma's Military Academy did not work out for my dad, he took an alternate path to bettering himself. He enrolled in the Cortez Peters Business School. Cortez Peters, Sr., opened the business schools in Washington DC, Baltimore, and Chicago. The schools were the first black-owned schools in the field and, during their years of operation trained approximately 45,000 students. Both father and son made careers out of teaching their craft to others. The tuition was reasonable and could be paid weekly. He registered for the commercial course and studied business administration. He subsequently earned certificates of membership in the Order of Gregg Artist in Shorthand and Typing. Florence E. Ulrich was chief examiner and Harold H. Smith was editor.

Simultaneously, my dad taught swimming at the Young Men's Christian Association (YMCA) and became a part-time stock porter at the Emerson Hotel. He eventually got full-time work at the Alcazar Hotel, starting as a busboy working from seven in the morning to seven at night, seven days a week and earning $7 per week. To hear this tale was unbelievable to me.

When I was in my forties, my dad told me the story of the death of his sister Rosalie. He was ten years old and was plagued by memories of that day for all of his teen and adult years. My dad felt responsible for his sister's death. I will share more on this story however it was an important part of his life as a child.

CHAPTER 3

An Early Marriage and Children

1939

After high school, my dad took an interest in girls. He wrote in his journal that one of his uncles retired from the Baltimore Postal Service and opened a lunchroom on the southwest corner of Division and Lanvale Streets. This block in the city was considered important at that time. Little Willie and Victorine Adams lived across the street. She was a schoolteacher. A schoolteacher in the African American community in those days was a status position; it implied a college education and regular income. My dad's aunt was the cook, and my dad was the dishwasher, his first job as such.

Through this job, he met Eva, a petite, well-built, and refined girl. My dad wrote that Eva's parents were very vigilant when he visited her at their home. Eva and my dad would sit on the sofa and talk, and sometimes steal a kiss. Eva's father made sure my dad was out of their house by 9:00 p.m.

My mother and her sister Agnes were born and raised in Washington DC. When Agnes, the younger sister, moved away from home to get away from her overbearing father, she moved to Baltimore to live with her aunt Willie and her husband. Her aunt Willie lived next door to Eva's parents. My dad's best buddy, Henry Harrell, dated Agnes.

Henry Harrell informed my dad that Agnes's sister from Washington DC was visiting Baltimore for the weekend. Her name was Zelma. When

21

she arrived, Henry Harrell and Agnes double-dated with Zelma and my dad.

From the first date, whenever Zelma visited her sister and aunt, my dad would cross the railing that divided the two porches of the Baltimore-style row houses. He would sit with Zelma. He said the rules were less strict at Zelma's aunt Willie's house. Eventually, my dad stopped seeing Eva and spent all of his time with Zelma.

Catholic schools taught my dad that sex before marriage and masturbation were sins. He had passed the age of his first erections and wet dreams. He was approaching twenty years of age, and his sex drive was strong. Girls had hugged and kissed him. They encouraged sex, but in his mind, it was a sin. His solution to having sex was to get married.

On November 17, 1939, he married Zelma, Agnes's older sister. There was no tuxedo or wedding gown. They were married by a Catholic priest. Zelma had to agree to raise any children that were produced in this marriage Catholic. She agreed. My dad took Zelma to his parents' house and told them they were married. They both had jobs and lived with his parents until they found housing of their own, which did not come until after the birth of their first child. My grandmother must have been a saint to have raised her six children and now grandchildren too. My grandmother always said she liked boy children; the girls were too hard to raise, and therefore my brother was adored as her first grandchild.

My mother and my father's first two children arrived one year apart, 1940 and 1941. My dad said that my mother's hair and skin were her crowning glories. Zelma was of fair complexion, like his mother's. Her hair was thick, shiny, and professionally curled. She, like Eva, was petite. Zelma was loquacious, and my dad found her to be very entertaining and a complement to his chronic quiet nature. Zelma kept things lively.

My mother reported in later years that my dad was drinking gin miniatures when she dated him, which was the only way to get him to talk. She said otherwise, he wouldn't say a word. She said that on their wedding night, they stayed in a hotel room at the Emerson Hotel where he had worked. They shared a pound of white grapes. The hotel room and the grapes were luxuries for them. She said my dad stood and looked out the window over the city most of the night. She said he looked forlorn. His work at the Alcazar was not earning him enough money to support a family, or the classical life he cherished as a student in Catholic school.

Of Time and Spirit

My dad remained deeply conflicted over his religious teachings and his physical nature. He wrote the following notes on scratch paper:

> Beginning marriage, no birth control, if ten or more, no problem. Sincere Catholic at start. Abortion a sin. Catholic, cult, creed, mass, every Sunday, holy days of obligation, parochial school, become altar boy, no idea of girls. When nature began to grab a hold, was told sex outside marriage a sin, masturbation a sin. After marriage adultery a sin, birth control a sin. If sex outside marriage creates (baby) pregnancy.

When I was this same age, none of this was on my mind as a Catholic, but it was taught to me.

On May 5, 1941, my dad was hired as a civilian at Edgewood Arsenal in Edgewood, Maryland. He worked in the chemical plant as a laborer. The Army Chemical Corps conducted classified human subject research at the Edgewood Arsenal facility in Maryland. The purpose was to study the effects of low-dose chemical warfare agents on military personnel. They also tested protective clothing, pharmaceuticals, and vaccines. The chemical agents tested on subjects included chemical warfare agents and other related agents. They included anticholinesterase nerve agents, mustard agents, nerve agent antidotes, nerve agent reactivators, psychoactive agents (including LSD and PCP), irritants and riot control agents, alcohol, and caffeine.

This was not a job my dad wanted, but the pay was good, and he figured he could eventually make a career as a civil service employee. The Glenn L. Martin Company was an American aircraft and aerospace manufacturing company that moved their headquarters from Cleveland, Ohio, to Baltimore. They were hiring colored laborers as well. They were paid substantially more money than the federal government but were offered fewer fringe benefits. Some of my dad's buddies were riding around in Cadillacs and Buicks, while my dad purchased used Chevrolets. My dad's buddies urged him to come work with them, but my dad declined. Glenn L. Martin was in Baltimore and closer to his home in Baltimore than Edgewood, but the army was more stable, and when the company went defunct in 1961, many of my dad's buddies were out of work. My dad made the smarter choice for himself. During this time, he had been skipped over by the Selective Service from being drafted in the army. He was classified a pre–Pearl Harbor father.

This job at Edgewood necessitated his taking the train from Baltimore's Penn Station to Edgewood, Maryland, each day. He did not like the commute or the distance between home and work, but he needed the money now, having a wife and one child. Living at home with his parents did not bother him, but it bothered my mother. She said, "It was too much commotion."

In a short time, my dad, my mother, and my brother moved from his parents' house in Baltimore to 18 Battle Street in Edgewood. This was a one-bedroom, one-level attached apartment. This was a federally owned segregated housing project for African Americans. It was designed to be temporary housing the army built for its active and civilian colored employees during the war years. There was a similar community across Trimble Road for whites. I was instructed as a child to never cross over to the white project. Edgewood was segregated, and the people were mostly poor and racist. In the city, it would have been called a ghetto, but in Edgewood, it was called a project.

My mother was ecstatic with the thought of living for the first time in her own quarters, as she called it. In her mind, military housing was a step up from urban public housing. She was not fond of some of the newer housing and urban development housing projects in Baltimore. She preferred to live farther out of the city for the sake of their children. This move was a win-win for my dad and my mother. My dad could reduce his commute time to almost nothing, and my mother could have a place of her own away from the congestion at her in-laws' and their remaining children that lived at home. It was overcrowding by today's standards.

Family and friends did not think it was wise for my mother to move so far away. Edgewood was thirty miles from the city. She was a mother of one and expecting another. They considered that her husband would be at work every day; there would be no one that she knew to call upon if she needed help. My mother, on the other hand, was determined to have her own space away from the crowded conditions of her in-laws. Although her second child was due in four months, she assured everyone that she would be OK. She and my dad proceeded with the move, and their second child was born in good health. They were happy.

In anticipation of the second child, my dad and my mother secured a two-bedroom apartment at 15-B Hartman Street in Edgewood. This apartment was on the same property and located literally up the hill from 18 Battle Street. They needed space to accommodate themselves and their two children.

When the Japanese bombed Pearl Harbor in December 1941, almost all able-bodied young men were being called to join the military. My dad was again passed over because he was considered a pre–Pearl Harbor father. My dad wanted to enlist in the army to be like other men who were serving their county. In keeping with his plans to attend Saint Emma's Military Academy, he also saw the opportunity of becoming an officer. An officer in the United States Army was about as good as it got during that period of American history for colored men.

My mother did not want him to enlist; her marriage was still new and she was pregnant. However, since it was something he wanted to do, she consented. She took credit for getting my dad in the army. Her consent made it possible for him to serve; her decision, however, left her alone with two babies to manage on her own. This was a daunting challenge, but she thought she could handle it, and she did manage alone very well.

The Selective Service local board 13 located at 882 Park Avenue, Baltimore, sent my dad a notice to appear for a physical examination on January 6, 1944. The notice came in the form of a letter to his new address at 18 Battle Street, postmarked December 3, 1943. He was happy. He had never been anywhere outside of Baltimore, and this was his chance to see the world. He was modeling his two uncles. He wanted to be just like them. He was twenty-five years old, he had only had one girlfriend, one wife, one child, and another on the way. My dad was a brave man. At twenty-five years old, I was still a mama's boy, never thinking of carrying such a heavy burden. This was the life he was creating from his limited exposure to life. This was an early marriage and early fatherhood for my dad.

25

CHAPTER 4

A Segregated United States Army

1944

Up to this point, my dad lived a segregated life. The neighborhood where he lived in Baltimore City, the Catholic church, Catholic school, and public high school he attended were all segregated. He was married now with one child and another on the way. He had never faced blatant and stand-up-in-your-face discrimination and racism until he enlisted in the segregated United States Army. He had earlier in his childhood suffered the pain of losing his baby sister in a house fire, a death he felt responsible for; and he had suffered the disappointment of not being able to attend the Saint Emma's Military Academy, located in Powhatan, Virginia, after completing Catholic school. Transitioning to the United States Army was yet another painful experience for him. There was prejudice, segregation, discrimination, and racism as he had never before experienced; and although legally a man, married, and with children, he was a sheltered man.

On January 29, 1944, my dad received order number 3586 to report for induction at 7:00 a.m. Major Donald Smith provided my dad with a reference letter to present to the reception center, advising that my dad had been employed by Edgewood Arsenal as a chemical plant operator since May 1941. Major Smith thought the letter essential because my dad had specialized military experience, although a civilian. The letter was

26

essentially useless at the time. The induction officer looked at the letter and stamped it "Infantry," a foot soldier.

In preparation for his entrance into the army, my dad did all he could to prepare his wife and their home for his departure. He chopped enough wood to last the entire winter. There was plenty of canned food on the food storage shelves; and the bread man, milk man, insurance man, and gas man were all paid up. He had saved enough money for my mother to live until her allotment checks arrived. He was precisely prepared for his transfer to the military. My mother always credited my dad for "taking care of business care."

My dad had never given a thought as a young man to the United States Army as being segregated. It was far from his mind that humans could be so cruel and noncaring. Similar to the transition from Catholic school to public schools, the transition from a civilian job to the United States Army was a huge leap for him. It was more traumatizing, but he maintained a level head, a positive attitude, and a sense of purpose. He wanted to be uplifted from his low-born economic and racial class.

His first experience with segregation occurred when he was called to take his physical examination. His examination was not completed on a nearby military base where white men took their examination. Instead, it was completed at Provident Hospital. It was the Baltimore hospital relegated to providing health care to coloreds. It never occurred to my dad that United States Army had separate facilities for coloreds to take their physical examination. My dad's physical examination results were stellar. His results were forwarded to the proper army personnel. Following his physical examination, he was to report to the main floor of the Fifth Regiment Armory at Hoffman and Bolton Streets in Baltimore.

My dad was inducted into the army as a Tec 4. He was twenty-five years old, a laborer at the chemical plant in Edgewood at his induction. The army recorded that my dad had brown eyes, black hair, and was "colored."

He completed seventeen weeks of basic infantry training at the Fifth Training Regiment, Infantry Replacement Training Center, Fort McClellan, Alabama, on July 1944. His rank was Private, Army specialty. When he had completed basic training, he was sent to Fort Meade, Maryland for two additional weeks of advance basic training.

Then followed thirteen weeks of combat training in Naples, Italy. This prepared him for frontline duty in Europe. He successfully learned to fire fifteen different rifles. They discovered in my dad's records that he could type, take shorthand, and perform clerical functions, skills he learned at night at the Cortez Peters Business School. The army immediately sent my dad instead to headquarters since few men of that day knew shorthand and typing. All the officers were white; the non-commissioned were colored. He never had to shoot any of the rifles that he was trained to use. He was a Clerk-typist (405) and an operations sergeant (814).

In my dad's notes, he described two incidents of racism when he traveled from Maryland to Alabama for basic training. He wrote,

> There was no separation of races on the train heading south from Baltimore, Maryland to Washington, DC. However, when we arrived in DC they put the colored men on separate cars going from DC to Alabama. I kept my mouth shut, as my father had instructed, but it was hard for to accept as true this was happening.

> During a stop in Columbia, South Carolina, I needed to board a bus to pick-up the next connecting train. When the bus stopped and the door opened, I attempted to enter the in front door of the bus. The driver, pulled the emergency brake to keep the bus from moving and jumped up immediately, grabbed an axe out of the emergency case and said: "You're one of those smart niggers." The colored passengers hollered go to the back door.

My dad was taken aback; he had never been treated so violently in his young life. It frightened him. He had a solid Christian background and had come from two devout Christian parents. He was a loyal believer in God. He possessed a classical education that included the music of Richard Wagner and the poetry of William Shakespeare. In South Carolina, on this day, it counted for nothing. My dad was still a "nigger" in the eyes of the white bus driver.

When he arrived at Fort McClellan, he was directed to report to Headquarters. Within the headquarters building, he had to drink at separate drinking fountains: "For whites only" and "For colored only." This was a new experience. He was shocked, humiliated, and demeaned;

Of Time and Spirit

and he had not yet gotten started with his lengthy stretch in the army that he volunteered to join.

My dad wrote the following in his journal:

Camp Shelby, Mississippi, I was in Fort Dix, New Jersey, a T/4 NCO in uniform. I was about to be shipped to Camp Shelby, Mississippi. There were five white privates in uniform. Being of the highest rank, and going to the same camp. I was put in charge. They put the records together with mine on top, and I was to present them to the Transportation Sargent who would meet us at the train depot. I arrived at the appointed time, as instructed, and the white privates were to follow me to the area where the military reported. I presented the records, as I was instructed, to the white Transportation Sergeant, also in military garb the same as mine.

He took the records from me and read the top one and said: "Who is Dorsey?"' I said: "I am." He took my records, put them on the bottom of the pile, turned to the privates, and said, "You all let this nigger bring you down here?" He then proceeded to call two buses, one for me and one for them.

He then told the bus driver that the white mess hall would prepare a meal for us. The privates were taken to the dining area, and the nigger would be served from the back door of the kitchen. It turned out that the mess sergeant was colored. He prepared hot dogs and beans for them, and a full-course steak dinner for me.

Then we boarded our respective buses and went our separate ways, I was delivered to the colored barracks, and instructed how colored soldiers were to act in Mississippi. We were truly treated like second-class citizens, in the United States Army.

After reading theses notes, I thought he was not only treated like a second-class citizen, or he was not treated like a human being. Treatment like this infuriates and creates hostilities that are cumulative and long lasting for African Americans.

In later years, when my dad would tell this story at many family gatherings, he would chuckle. In my mind, there was no way he could have ever thought this situation was funny or slightly humorous. As far as I was concerned, he must have felt the pain and anguish. It was not funny. This was his method, I presume, to camouflage his pain. He always advised me, as his father advised him, "Learn to keep your mouth shut when you go into the army and don't volunteer for anything." I failed my father rather often in the category of keeping my mouth shut.

My dad also wrote in his journal,

> *B&O Railways in B'more, no segregation, changed at Washington to take trains south, put in front car which was directly behind engine, and coal car, seats and sills covered w/ coal dust. When trains became electric, we went to the back. The dining car had one corner for colored. When you were seated and began eating they pulled a curtain around the area, so whites did not have to watch you chew.*

My dad thought this humorous too. I did not. Perhaps this was his mode of coping.

At each location my dad was sent, they reviewed his clerical education and experience with incredulity, since there were few men with such skills, and a colored man to boot. He was placed as clerk-typist and operations sergeant, assigned to headquarters in each military base he was transferred to. This was considered a great position for a colored at the time. His successful completion of courses in shorthand and typing at the Cortez Peters Business School earlier kept him from the frontlines of the war. My dad was not shot up, disabled, or dead as a result of his military duty.

My dad also had the opportunity to teach swimming at Fort McClellan, a skill he learned at the Frederick Douglass High School. His previous experience as instructor at Frederick Douglas and the YMCA served the army well. At this stage of his military service, he received the EAME and Good Conduct medals. The EAME Medal stood for the European-African-Middle Eastern Campaign. It is an award of the United States Armed Forces, which was first created on November 6, 1942, by Executive Order 9265 issued by President Franklin D. Roosevelt. The medal was intended to recognize those military service members who had performed military duty in the European theater during the years of the Second

Of Time and Spirit

World War. These recognitions were in keeping with the same types he received in Catholic and public schools. My dad liked recognition for a job well done at a very early age. He enjoyed the challenge of learning.

On December 1, 1944, my dad received orders to report to Fort George G. Meade, Maryland, for assignments overseas. There were a total of eight men on this trip. No private vehicles, dependents, or relatives could accompany the men. Handbags or personal effects could not exceed the limit. If there was overage, it would be sent home at the government's expense at the permanent address on record.

The men had been trained and had received their last ration in the morning of December 1, 1944. No sack lunch was prepared, carried on, or packed with their baggage. The uniform that was to be worn were class A woolen with khaki shirt, overseas cap with blue piping. All barracks bags were stenciled and picked up by the baggage officer at central baggage and loaded on the train two hours prior to scheduled departure time. No handbags were checked.

John Tooker, plant supervisor from my dad's former job at Edgewood Arsenal, sent a second letter of support for my dad to his commanding officer in October 1944, which arrived prior to my dad's overseas assignment. It read,

To Whom It May Concern:

James R. Dorsey, Sr. worked at Edgewood Arsenal for over two years, and during part of that time he was responsible to me for job performed.

At all times, he was an able, dependable, and conscientious worker who never grumbled about assignments, and who was always endeavoring to better his status. His efforts were finally rewarded when he was promoted to Chemical Plant Operator shortly before he left for the Armed Forces.

For obvious reasons, his duties must remain secret but it will suffice to say that he was able to operate competently in a chemical and filling plant and I would recommend him highly for any work in the Chemical Warfare Service of this nature. John Tooker Plant Superintendent.

The letter landed on deaf ears. My dad was sent overseas to Livorno, Italy, for twelve weeks of combat training.

My dad, Private James R. Dorsey, Sr., was to proceed on or about August 1, 1945, from the present station to the Fifth Army Rest Center in Florence, Italy, for a period of seven days. After my dad's arrival in Florence, Italy, he was assigned to the headquarters of the Forty-Ninth Quartermaster Group, by special orders 146 by Colonel Bumen, John W. Moore, first lieutenant.

In 1945, he was offered more money and a bonus if he agreed to reenlist, or re-up, as they called it, thus he was honorably discharged on October 29, 1945, Livorno, Italy, signed by John T. McKee, lieutenant colonel.

The State of Maryland, Executive Department Annapolis, Maryland, presented my dad with a Certificate of Appreciation for his service rendered while in the Armed Forces of the United States during World War II, signedArmy of Herbert R. O'Conor, governor of the State of Maryland.

My dad reenlisted in the army the next day, October 30, 1945. He was grade TEC 4. He had worked for nine months as a clerk typist and for five months in operations. He was credited with four years of high school, graduating Frederick Douglas High School in 1937 with academic diploma. He was also credited with twenty-one months of commercial courses in business administration from Cortez Peters School (1938–1939). While in Italy, my dad had become proficient in Italian. My mother was not happy about his reenlistment. She did not think he was going to be fool enough to re-up for two more years when she was at home alone with two children.

On November 22, 1945, my dad was furloughed until December 1, 1945. He returned home, where he resided at 15 Hartman Street, Edgewood. This was where my mother, my brother, and my sister lived while he was overseas. His next assignment was France, where he received: The Army of Occupation of Germany Medal. This is a military award of the United States military, which was established by the United States War Department on April 5, 1946. The medal was created in the aftermath of the Second World War to recognize those who had performed occupation service in either Germany, Italy, Austria, or Japan. The original Army Occupation Medal was intended only for members of the United States Army but was expanded in 1948 to encompass the United States Air Force shortly after that service's creation. The navy and marine equivalent of

Of Time and Spirit

the Army of Occupation Medal is the Navy Occupation Service Medal. My dad also received the American Theater European-African-Middle Eastern and Good Conduct Awards (both for a second time). My dad was in France from April 15, 1946, to June 1, 1946.

In July of 1946, my dad received an outstanding performance appraisal demonstrating high-quality leadership. He was recommended for Officer Candidate School. This was his goal and a dream come true for him. His character was rated excellent. His commanding officer wrote,

I have carefully considered the technical requirements of a second lieutenant of the arm of service for which the application is being made and believe that the applicant possesses educational qualifications of practical experience which will enable him to complete satisfactory the course of instruction at the Officer Candidate School (OCS). My dad's Army General Classification Test Score was 112 thus my dad's request was approved and signed by Joseph W. Cushman Captain Infantry, and Thomas R. Hoag, Lieutenant Colonel, July 31, 1946.

In August of 1946, my dad requested authorization to attend the next course for Officer's Candidate School, held in Camp Lee, Virginia, beginning August 26, 1946. He requested his appointment in the Quartermaster Corps.

He was again required to complete a Personal Qualifications Questionnaire and physical examination. At this time, he was on a class A detail to Aberdeen Proving Ground, Maryland, assigned to Battalion Headquarters as General Clerk. Captain Joseph W. Cushman was his immediate supervisor. The Aberdeen Proving Ground location was just a short distance from Edgewood Arsenal. This location was much closer to home. He also enrolled in a correspondence course that taught radio practice and theory. This was an eighteen-month program.

My dad first completed the Annual Physical Examination for OCS. The report showed he had no illnesses, no injuries, no operations, no chronic diseases or allergies in the past five years. His vision was 20/200 correctible in both the right and left eyes. His hearing was normal; nose and throat normal; good posture; cardiovascular system normal; respiratory system normal; chest x-ray normal; skin and lymphatics normal; bone, joints, muscles normal; abdominal viscera normal; hernia and hemorrhoids none;

genitourinary system normal; nervous system normal; lab test negative; corrective measures none. Is the individual incapacitated? No. Does he meet physical requirements? Yes.

My dad received a letter from the Ordnance Training Center, Aberdeen Proving Ground, Maryland, that read,

> *On August 16, 1946, you were examined by the Officer Candidate School Board, this headquarters, and found qualified for admission into Quartermaster Corps Officer Candidate School.*

On August 21, 1946, the Ordnance Training Center sent a transmittal of OCS application to the Adjutant General, War Department, Washington DC, that read,

> *OCS application and allied papers of T/4 James R. Dorsey, 33904428, who has been provisionally accepted for Quartermaster Corps." Signed William L. Waller, Major, Ordnance Department.*

My dad was anticipative, for he knew he was still colored, and only a precious few coloreds made officer.

On September 16, 1946, the War Department, the Adjutant General's Office, Washington DC, wrote to the Commanding General, Ordnance Training Center, Aberdeen Proving Ground, Maryland:

> *The application and allied papers of T/4 James R. Dorsey for Army Officer Candidate School are returned herewith. Applicant does not meet visual requirement of paragraph . . . for commission in services of the Reserve Components. BY ORDER OF THE SECRETARY OF WAR.*

When my dad received the news, it was an enormous disappointment. It was professed by some whites that as a colored, by dad had a "plum" spot working in the headquarters; for a Negro to aim high was a penalty. By September 23, 1946, my dad was transferred from headquarters to another location and duty assignment. He was defeated.

Of Time and Spirit

On September 25, 1946, under advisement, my dad resubmitted his application and Allied papers for Officer Candidate School for consideration as an officer in another division with an approval recommendation from his commanding officer James T. Wright, with a note: "Attention is invited to preceding endorsement."

In the meantime, the war in Europe had ended. My dad and other combat-trained infantrymen were boarded on ships to what was to be the invasion of Japan. While on the way, the atomic bombs were dropped, and their orders were changed.

In restricted communications from the Ordnance Training Center at Aberdeen Proving Ground, Maryland, October 9, 1946, my dad received news that under special orders, he was being transferred to Camp Stoneman, California, to the overseas replacement depot. He was once again denied acceptance to OCS. This second rejection demolished his spirits for OCS.

On October 11, 1946, my dad wrote his commanding officer requesting that his name be removed from the Special Orders for overseas duty pending the outcome of request for dependency discharge. I think my dad felt unjustly treated regarding his rejection from OCS. He saw no future in the army, thus his new aim was to get out of the army.

On October 14, 1946, my dad made the request to be discharged from the army, providing the following justification:

> I am 27 years old and enlisted on October 30, 1945. I am attached unassigned and performing duty as cadre. Prior to enlistment, I was employed by Chemical War-fare Service, Edgewood Arsenal Maryland. I was not deferred by Selective Service for dependency. I did not appeal my classification. I have applied for discharge from the Army of the United States for Dependency due to hardship. My wife and two children are solely dependent upon me for support. My wife is now pregnant. My wife lives in the country. The nearest stores are almost a mile away. During this coming winter, my wife will experience undue hardships in caring for our home and children unless I am discharged. Due to the crowded conditions of hospitals my wife has to travel from Edgewood, Maryland to Baltimore, Maryland, a distance of twenty-five miles for treatment. Every time she goes anywhere she has to carry the two children or pay

35

someone to keep them. If conditions continue to progress in this manner it will seriously impair the health of my wife.

On December 13, 1946, my dad was honorably discharged from the army and presented a certificate for honest and faithful service to the United States, given at Camp Stoneman, California, signed by Major Ray Turner. My dad was out of the army, and I was to be born in May 1947.

In looking over my dad's timeline, I could not help but wonder if my conception was a result of his OCS rejections, considering that my mother repeatedly said she never wanted to have me and she was not happy with his reenlistment. She had strong desires to start working out of the home. She and my dad agreed she could not work out of the home until the last child was in first grade. Then I was born, and she had to wait another six years before she could go to work. She was not happy about being pregnant again.

Although my mother was the bedrock of my life, I was affected for decades by her harpings of never wanting to have me. If my wonderment is true, it explains the many years I felt unloved by both parents. For my mother, it was another six to seven years of deferment of her career, and for my dad, I was an opportunity to be discharged from the army. I will never know.

The army was my dad's first introduction to the reality of segregation, prejudice, and institutionalized racism. He was one of many Negro soldiers who were mistreated while serving their country. I am proud he survived and sad that his dreams of becoming an officer never came true. To this day, I cannot comprehend the United States Army being segregated. Reprehensible!

On July 26, 1948, President Harry S. Truman signed this executive order establishing the president's committee on Equality of Treatment and Opportunity in the Armed Services, committing the government to integrating the segregated military. Although it took more than six years to fully implement, this action set in motion reforms not only in the military but in the federal workforce and public education. My dad's birth order once again stopped him from pursuing his dreams of becoming an officer in the United States Army, by this time it was too late, but he was still not deterred from making a successful life for himself.

CHAPTER 5

Civilian Career Launch and Family Life

1947

After being discharged from the army, my dad did not know where his passions were regarding his career or life. He had married, as the Catholic Church prescribed, and had children. His aspirations of becoming an officer were truncated three times: once with his lost opportunity to attend to St. Emma's Military Academy, and twice in the army (OCS). He returned to his job at the Army Chemical Center in Edgewood, Maryland. He earned three times the amount of money compared to what he had earned when he started in 1941. He had three additional years of experience and exposure to a larger world through his military experiences.

His first attempt at finding himself professionally was to enroll in a radio theory correspondence course offered by the National Radio Institute. His veteran's benefits paid for this training. He successfully completed this course and submitted his certification of completion to the Veterans Benefits Administration at 1315 St. Paul Street, Baltimore, on March 10, 1947. His completion certificate was signed by R. T. Brown, acting chief of the Vocational Rehabilitation and Education Division then located on Sixteenth and U Streets, NW Washington DC.

My dad revealed to my mother that while he was in the army, he had casual sex with French, Italian, and German women while overseas. Like a good Catholic, he wanted to confess his sins to her as he was taught. It seems to me that his good Catholic teachings failed him, as did his libido,

37

while separated from his wife and children. This confession did not sit well with my mother. She was pregnant with a third child that he wanted and she did not. She got pregnant for him. She never wanted to have another child. His confession added fuel to her wanting to jumpstart a career of her own. She was from Washington DC, where women were being employed by the federal government as a result of President Truman's integration of the armed forces. During the war and after, women were entering the workforce. She wanted her own money. She had witnessed too many men leaving their wives for other women. She was already aware of the interest some women had in her husband, my father. She was thinking ahead just in case she was stuck in the same situation, with three children and no man.

My mother was the type of woman who thought sex was overrated. She would say, "A woman has to clean up before and after sex while the man is sleeping soundly afterwards." There was no love and affection for the woman. She would bellow, "Women are sorry creatures!" His confession did not help his case with her, perhaps with God, for telling the truth. My mother never anticipated my dad's infidelities. She was not a happy camper. I am sure she, or any man or woman receiving such a confession would be happy, pleased, or thrilled. Maybe this is why she repeatedly told me she never wanted to have me. She may have been angry. This was her confession to me for years. Her confession to me did not sit well with me just as my dad's was not pleasant for her. I had nothing to do with my creation, but she was my mother, she was definitely my life's backbone. She was dutiful as a wife and a mother beyond my conception or understanding.

To add further insult to her pregnancy, on May 7, 1947, three days before I was born, my dad broke his leg by jumping out of a moving car. After being examined and having his leg set in a cast at the hospital, he was transported to the nearest location, which was his mother and father's house in Baltimore, where he and my mother once lived after they got married. My mother was pregnant in Edgewood, twenty-five to thirty miles away, due to deliver her child at any moment, and no husband to help with the delivery of the child he wanted. In my adult years, she told me, "I was fit to be tied!"

For my mother, this meant she was charged solely for packing up her two children, transporting them to a neighbor for babysitting, boarding a bus while in labor, and traveling twenty-five miles to get to the Provident Hospital for colored people by way of bus. She was alone. She felt betrayed and disgusted. She was not happy with the birth of this baby. As an adult, I understood.

After her arrival at the hospital, she was ejected due to an outbreak of polio in the maternity ward. She then went to her mother-in-law's house, where my dad was recuperating from his broken leg. When she arrived, she said to my dad, "I guess I will have my baby here."

My grandmother quickly interjected: "There will be no baby born in here tonight!"

"Well, Ma?" my mother cried. "Where am I supposed to go?"

My grandmother said, "Go to your sister's house. She lives a few blocks away."

My mother was crestfallen; she was ejected from the hospital and now ejected from my grandmother's house. My grandmother said, "I will get two of the children to walk you over there." My grandmother's side of the family were described as stoic. I call it cold, but times were extremely difficult for colored people then too!

Tired, heartbroken, deflated, and in labor, my Uncle Maurice and Aunt Theresa walked my mother to her sister Agnes's apartment. I was eventually born at 8:00 a.m. on May 10, the Saturday before Mother's Day, at my Aunt Agnes's apartment located at 1016 Fulton Avenue, Baltimore, Maryland.

Dr. I. Bradshaw Higgins said to my mother after I was born, "Name?"

Sedated, my mother replied, "What?"

"What is your child's name?"

My mother was so disgusted she said to my Aunt Theresa, "Name the boy!"

At that moment, my mother did not care about my name. She thought she had gone through all of this suffering for my dad, and he was not even present for the delivery of the child he said he wanted to have. It had been a miserable few days for her. Under the circumstances, I would not have wanted to have another baby either.

It was a dreadful pregnancy and dreadful delivery. My mother said to me years later that I came out smiling; but she swore to her creator that she would never have another child. It was known by then she did not want the baby. I would guess she was not too happy with my dad at that time. You think?

39

My mother was totally upset that my dad made no effort to be present for the delivery. She said to my dad, "You could have at least made some effort to be present, considering all I went through to get here."

My dad's reply was, "Women have been having babies for hundreds of years. I didn't see why I needed to be there."

My mother's retort was, "Yes! But they were not having *your* child!"

My mother stayed furious with my dad for years and recalled the story over and over, year in and year out.

I can't say the world welcomed my birth. It felt to me that nobody wanted to see me coming! I have thought over later years after repeatedly hearing this story, I was Whoopi Goldberg in the movie *The Color Purple*: in the scene where Harpo tells her that she is ugly and she retorts, "But I am here!"

The address 20 Battle Street is an appropriate street address for a military property. It was the first home that I knew. This was a third move for our family. This was a three-bedroom apartment. There were three children now. My sister was housed in the largest bedroom. My brother and I were cramped into the smallest bedroom. My mother and my father had the bedroom on the front, which was middle size. It too was the same segregated military housing project where my family lived before my birth. I grew up in this apartment until I was in third grade. It was the most barren plot of land I ever recall seeing. It was bordered by a small forest of trees that separated the white community from the colored community. The cinderblock apartments were painted in drab military colors. There was no landscaping of any type. The units were four or five attached apartments with one-bedroom end units that were entered from the side of the building. When it rained, the water erosion washed away the top soil to the point some yards were red clay and stones. Cars were parked on the street in no semblance of order. The men, who were truck drivers, would drive their dump trucks on the gravel roads, pressuring the top gravel to the curbs. Although military housing, it was really just a step up from a trailer park I thought. For the most part, the people got along, and most minded their business. There was one public telephone booth located in the center of the enclave for families with no telephone. Neighbors stood in line to use the telephone. The telephone booth was often the scene of an argument if someone stayed on the telephone too long, such as a teen talking to their boy or girl friends in secret, their parents not knowing of their plans to rendezvous.

Of Time and Spirit

Our neighborhood was comprised of colored military families who came from different post around the world and were stationed at Edgewood for short periods of time before being transferred out to some other United States post or foreign assignment. Our apartment always stood out to me as one of the nicer ones because my mother planted multicolored zinnias along the front sidewalk, and there were matching white sheer curtains on the front of the house, giving a sense of uniformity to the exterior of our house. My mother, who grew up economically poor, had exquisite taste in home furnishing from her exposure to Washington DC townhouses. This was an outcome of her working in the homes of a white congressman as a child laborer. This was before there were child labor laws; and if the laws were in place, they would not have protected colored children anyway.

I suspect that my mother and my father came to some measure of accord after I was born. My mother was a stay-at-home mother to me while my brother and my sister attended a one-room school in Magnolia. My dad made little of his needs to provide for his children. My mother would say that my dad would accept anything she purchased for the children but didn't want her to have the least little thing.

I remember the icebox placed against the front wall of the cramped kitchen, and the iceman bringing a huge block of ice every few days to keep the food cold. The icebox was an ugly contraption, and water dripped everywhere when the ice was delivered. My mother was always running behind the iceman, wiping up the water from the dripping ice to keep from losing the glow of the Johnson's Glo-Coat Floor Wax she or my dad put down every two weeks on the linoleum covered floors. We seemed to get a new piece of patterned linoleum to cover the black and brown asphalt tiles that were installed on the floor with the construction of the small apartments. My dad laid each roll of linoleum. Sometimes the linoleum was larger than the space it was purchased for. My dad would get on his hands and knees to cut it to fit around the walls and around the appliances. My mother watched and specified a neat cut and edge. My dad always did a great job at making the floors look better.

I remember the potbellied stove that sat in the living room. It warmed the entire three-bedroom apartment. We had a wood stove in the kitchen where my mother cooked breakfast, lunch, and dinner every day. The same stove was used to heat a straightening comb for my sister's hair and touch up her own.

41

When I was a child, my mother would have me put spit on my index finger and instructed me to touch the hot metal skirt that surrounded the stove, and she would teach me "Hot!" I learned that lesson rather quickly and moved cautiously when near the hot stoves. The stoves were bulky and took up considerable space in rather small rooms, but they gave us heat during the winter months. We were never cold.

Since my dad did not want my mother to work outside of the home, she took in ironing and babysitting for extra money. She said that of all the household chores, she liked ironing most; and she could spend hours ironing. She called it "ironing up a storm!"

While my dad made his needs minimal, my mother did not. I recall her purchasing our first Tappan Range and Frigidaire refrigerator. Each time my mother purchased a new appliance, on the delivery date, my dad would bark, "That thing is not coming in here!" But it did.

Although she continued to get his payroll checks and managed the household finances, she would retort, "I brought this with my own money." She would lament that she had to pinch from the food money to get pair of drawers for herself. It could have been true, but my mother had a tendency to exaggerate too. These situations assuredly escalated my mother's desire to have a job out of the home because she did not want some man telling her what she could and could not purchase. She was determined to someday get a job out of the home.

In 1949, my dad purchased the first family car. It was a used 4-door 1947 Chevrolet Fleetmaster. The cost was $1,395.00. There was no trade-in and there was $511.15 cash down payment. With insurance and other costs, his payments were $57.04/month for twenty-one months. My dad hated debt. My mother did not care about debt. She consistently claimed over the years that she purchased the car, but in those days, women could not get credit in their name, thus the car was put in my dad's name; and legally, it was his car. My dad did not resist her wanting a car, but she was indeed the principal driver. As with every material thing we had my mother had to beg, argue, or cajole to get it in the house. My dad was not a materialistic man; he did not like the accumulation of material things.

I recall the first detachment from my dad when I was three to four years old. I would run to him when he came home from work so I could be hugged or picked up, just like he described his baby sister Rosalie. He always said to me, "Get down, boy!" Or "Go away!" My feelings would be hurt, and eventually, I stopped running to him. I was much too young to know if he had a bad day or that life just wasn't good to him at that time. It was probably both. Regardless, I took it as rejection and stayed out of his way. In the years that followed, I learned and I continued to stay out of his way. Eventually, I understood that he was an unfulfilled man and was still trying to find himself and seeking his level of inner peace.

When I was about five years old, my dad purchased for me an extra-large blue tricycle. The tricycle was almost too large for me to pedal. I did not ride it that much. My mother said it was a waste of money because she could never get me to go outside of the house to play. She complained, "All he wants to do is stick up under me!" I was accustomed to being in the house all day with her as she systematically managed our house. She talked to me all day long, incessantly. I wasn't lonely. Being with my mother was totally entertaining for me. She was constantly teaching me something about washing, ironing, cooking, polishing the furniture or silver plate flatware or serving pieces. Or something as simple as handing her clothespins as she hung wet clothes on the clothesline. Through every chore, she was talking to me or telling a story. I learned my numbers, colors, the alphabet, spelling, and counting money. All types of teaching took place in these activities. I got praise for my help, and praise was important to me.

In addition, there was a six-and seven-year difference between me and my siblings. They were almost teenagers, and certainly of the age of not wanting to be bothered with a baby brother. As a result, I learned to do things on my own. This was a mixed blessing from the standpoint that I didn't have any friends. Therefore, the tricycle my dad purchased was practically new when my mother eventually gave it away. She continued to complain it was a waste of money. She seldom liked anything he bought for the children or the house; she declared the house and the children were her domain. There was no space in the house to store my tricycle,

I remember attending church as a family at the Post Chapel at Edgewood Arsenal. It never seemed to be a happy time, as I recall. It seemed to me everybody was irritable, and logically so, living in cramped quarters with one bathroom for everyone to get ready in time to go to Catholic Mass. My mother hated going to Catholic services at the start of her marriage because Mass was delivered in Latin, and she didn't know what the priest was saying. Moreover, she hated getting out of bed in the morning in general, and to attend a Latin Mass was useless to her. The church was segregated, and colored people were relegated to the gallery of the church or the choir loft. Coloreds were not welcomed in the main sanctuary of the church.

During the summer months, it was hot and sticky in the balcony of the chapel, and with a white shirt, tie and blazer, it was oppressive. I was restless and couldn't sit still. The services were so solemn it was like being in a tomb. My mother would place her arm around me and hold me close in her armpit to keep me sitting up and straight. She would, inaudibly say to me that Mass would be over soon. The service was only forty-five minutes to an hour, yet the entire family seemed to be simply going through the motions and waiting for it to be over. Instructions by the priest to stand, kneel, and sit helped to break the excruciating monotony. The rituals of the Catholic Church were choreographed.

Some Sundays, I would break away from my parents and run to the front row of the chapel. The dense, plush red carpet felt so good under my feet. I would sit in the row reserved for the officers, their wives, and children. I never knew that I was prohibited from being seated in the area reserved for whites only. As a child, I did not see myself as any different, nor did I know and understand segregation.

My parents would not retrieve me for fear of disturbing the peace or for being viewed as coloreds making a scene in the house of God. My dad would softly inform me after church, "Maurice, it is better to sit in the back of the church and be called forward than to sit in the front of the church and be told to go to the back."

I did not know what he meant and continued to sit in the front when I could escape the clutches of my mother's hand. I was never told to go to the back of the church. I was always clean and well-dressed in a way that represented my mother. Mentally, my dad was coming from his segregated Catholic Church experiences from his generation. My dad would tenderly but disapprovingly say to my mother, since she was in charge of the children, "That child does whatever he wants to do." It bothered him that I had so much freedom.

My mother was born Methodist and never enjoyed the Catholic Church. She complained about Mass being delivered in Latin and never understanding a word of what was being said. She would insist, "It is almost like not going to church." But while at home all day with my mother, I listened to her play her Wings over Jordan Gospel Choir 78 RPM recordings while cleaning the house. She would wrap her hair in a white baby diaper and sing along with the recordings at the pitch of her voice: "Touch Me Lord Jesus" and "My Soul just Couldn't Be Contented until I Found the Lord." When my siblings returned from school and my father returned from work, the house was clean. I was bathed and ready for bedtime, and she was showered and dressed.

At dinnertime, my dad sat at the head of the table, but it was the worst seat. It was in the corner of the kitchen. He sat with us for every meal. He used to hurry my mother to the table to eat after she finished cooking dinner, as she tried to tidy the kitchen before sitting down. He would nag: "Come on Zelma and sit down before the food gets cold!" When my mother finally got seated at the table he would say to all of us: "Now let's say grace." He would lead the table blessing: *"Bless us O Lord for these thy gifts which we are about to receive from thy bounty through Christ, our Lord. Amen.* Now let's eat!" My dad was hungry. I recall, for an example, if my mother prepared a whole chicken for dinner, he allowed the children to choose the part that they enjoyed most. My brother chose the drumsticks; he liked the dark meat. My sister chose the wings. My mother chose the breast, and I shared hers, and my father always ate what was left. He always wanted us to eat what we wanted. I never recall him saying "I love you" to any of us, but his actions most often put us first. Every Friday, our house smelled of fried fresh fish. Fish every Friday was yet another order of the Catholic Church. When food was discovered in the see, the Vatican created a rule for Catholics to support the seafood industries, where they also had money invested. This rule changed over time. The fish odor remained in our house until midday on Saturday. The odor was in the upholstery and draperies, and if you went out of the house and came back in, it was worse.

My dad always scolded the children when he would reach into a loaf of bread and the two end pieces of crusty bread, which he called "the heel of the bread," were face-to-face. My dad would eat those too; neither he nor my mother liked food wasted. My dad chanted, "Take what you want, but eat it all." My mother chanted, "You live in waste and die in want!" We heard about the starving children in other parts of the world too. Mealtime was yet another opportunity to instill home training.

My dad built a homemade workstation at the foot of the bunk beds my brother and I shared. It was snuggly jammed in the corner between the bed's footboard and the wall. It was homemade and custom-made. The desk portion of the work area had protractors, rulers, slide rules, pencils, graph paper, paperclips, stapler, pens, and ink all neatly organized. At night, after my sister washed the dinner dishes and my brother took out the trash and swept the kitchen floor and I was in bed for the night by 8:00 p.m., I could hear him when he entered our bedroom. When he turned on the light, it would awaken me, but I knew this was his time and not to whisper a word. I did not know what he was studying, but I knew he studied at his workstation all during the night, night after night. He was studying to get ahead, I suspected.

On weekends, my dad would cook a vanilla custard to go along with Jell-O—cherry or strawberry, rarely orange—that my mother made for dessert. The custard was alternately used for cakes my mother baked. My dad slowly settled into helping my mother with the children upon his return from the army. If she asked for help, he would pitch in. My dad was also engaged with the PTA. For a man of his generation, and in a military setting to boot, this was huge. Most of the men that I was exposed to worked while the wives ran the house and the children. A man who helped his wife was considered weak, but my dad was his own man, and he was always at home with us.

There were not too many family days out of the house—maybe one picnic in Druid Hill Park which always seemed to turn chaotic because of the impatience of one family member or the other. I did not like sitting outside to eat because of the flying or crawling bugs. I was an in-the-house child. One-half of the time we were outside, we were fanning away flies. My siblings appeared to have a love-hate relationship with each other; they were always fighting each other and seemed to love each other no end. Being the youngest of all my family members, I felt detached from everyone during these times. I was too young to be old and too old to be a baby. I hated these times and felt left out because when I opened my mouth to speak, my mother or my father would say, "Shut your mouth, boy!" Every chastisement was punctuated at the end with the word *boy*.

At Christmastime, my mother reported that my dad would stay up all night long, assembling the toys for the children that she shopped on weekends to buy. She would drive the 1947 Chevy to Baltimore to shop at Hecht's, Hochschild Kohn's, and Hutzler's department stores in downtown Baltimore. I loved riding in the front seat of the car, just my mother and me. When the whole family traveled, I was cramped between my mother and my father in the front or cramped in the back seat between my sister and my brother.

These were the premier department stores in Baltimore at the time. Before these stores were integrated, we had a very fair-complexed aunt who would go into the stores, passing for white, and would buy clothes for all the women in the family. The salesclerks thought my aunt was a rich white woman because she purchased so many dresses during the Christmas and Easter holidays. My aunt never told the salesladies any different. Some Negros at the time would boycott stores that segregated against them. When whites moved to the suburbs and needed Negro shoppers downtown, they integrated the stores. My mother welcomed the opportunity to shop in the better-quality stores. She tired of spending her money at the low-end stores and purchasing clothing that fell apart after several wearings. Hecht's was the first of the department stores to integrate, Hochschild Kohn's and Hutzler's followed. It was really fashionable to carry the Baltimore Shopper's plate, which was a small wallet-sized silver-colored metal plate that could be notched for all three stores. Steward's was the higher-end department store in Baltimore, and it was the last to integrate and the first to go out of business. Negros refused to patronize Stewart's after white flight to the suburbs. Stewart's closed in 1978; Hochschild Kohn's declared bankruptcy in 1984; Hutzler's liquidated in 1990; and Hecht's was acquired by Macy's and Bloomingdale's circa 2006. My mother and I shopped those stores until they closed.

My mother said my dad would sip his gin as he assembled the toys on Christmas Eve. Each of the children received department store toys and under- and outerwear for Christmas. My dad marveled as his children opened their Christmas gifts with such excitement and glee. He approved of my mother's selection of toys. My dad would say, "Zelma, gets those children the best of everything." My mother spent months making fruitcakes and prepping food for the holidays. I thought we had big Christmases, plenty of everything. My dad provided for us, for my mother was still not working out of the home at this point. I don't recall him getting anything special for Christmas. He made himself second at Christmastime for his children. He and my mother exchanged gifts in private. He usually gave her money, for he said that was the only thing that excited her. She got him underwear and pajamas. She lamented that he never brought himself anything and she was tired of washing and ironing his rags. He was appreciative and would chuckle to my mother. He cared less about wearing rags.

I discerned at about five years old that my dad was someone important. It was in 1951 and 1952 that his career was just beginning to take off. He had graduated Catholic school and graduated from one of the best colored high schools in the state of Maryland. He had completed a correspondence course in radio theory, a twenty-one-month course at Cortez Peters Business School. He had an honorable discharge from the army with a sterling record and was hired back by Edgewood Arsenal in the chemical plant. These fragments of his life filtered down in my childhood mind that my dad was somehow notable. This was not as great as some colored men, but it was very good during the time, and my dad's works were showing a progression upward.

His supervisors at Edgewood Arsenal recognized his talents; they valued them and used them to the government's advantage. In addition, he was always on time, and he consistently maintained a great attitude. Federal government leadership started to send my dad out of state for specialty training. This was a big deal in the now Negro community. There was a transition from colored to Negro somewhere during this era. He was first assigned to the Fundamentals of Electronics and Radio and Television Servicing at De Forest's Training in Chicago, Illinois (1951); Principles and Maintenance of Foxboro Instruments in Foxboro, Massachusetts (1953 and again in 1957); and the Bristol Company in Waterbury, Connecticut (1959). This was big for our family and the surrounding Negro community. Our neighbors had never heard of a Negro getting these types of professional opportunities in government. Although I did not know what esteem was at age five, I felt esteemed by my dad's out-of-state travels, I guess because my mother was so proud and supportive of his upward professional movement. Some men of his era did not have the same educational opportunity, white or Negro. My dad was being chosen over white men who worked in his division. This was extraordinary that he was selected.

My dad dressed to go to work in business clothes; I never knew that a chemical operator was considered a laborer when his white counterparts were called engineer associates. Although my dad had been assigned to headquarters while in the army and had performed a wide array of clerical duties, he returned to the chemical plant because the job paid more and he had a family to support. In the beginning, he worked swing shifts, twelve to eight, four to twelve, and eventually, he was promoted permanently to an eight to four-thirty schedule. He was regularly promoted and recommended for advanced technical training. My mother had the job of rotating her household functions when my dad worked swing shifts. My siblings and I all lived through and survived my dad's travels and swing shifts.

Of Time and Spirit

My dad gained continued respect by his supervisors and most peers. A Negro during this era was seldom awarded the same opportunities as the white workers. When my dad was assigned to training in Foxboro, Massachusetts, he was challenged by prejudice and discrimination. Airline travel was expensive—a luxury and a privilege reserved for whites. Few Negros traveled by this means of transportation. My dad was not fully welcomed by the airline or the passengers, but he was there on the airplane with other white people. Unknowingly, he was representing his race in yet another fight for equality. His method of fight was by modeling appropriate behavior and not conforming to prejudged stereotypes. He was being sponsored by the federal government, thus there wasn't much that could be said by anyone.

Once he arrived in Boston, he was met with prejudice at Foxboro Training and Education division. My dad was the only Negro in the class of nineteen. From a photograph I have, he was not seated in back but to the side of the room. He never sat in the front and asked to go to the back as he chided me in church, nor did he sit in the back. When the hotel accommodations were made, there was no room reserved for my dad, thus they moved my dad to a room in a private home of a white family. My dad was assigned to the homeowner's daughter's bedroom. My dad wrote, "He came out better than them. Private bath, private toilet, but had to use the back door of the house."

Upon completing the training courses, he was awarded with a certificate of satisfactory completion. Upon his return to work, he applied what he had learned to his job. My dad's supervisors were impressed with his learning and his ability to apply what he had learned with such accuracy, yielding successes for the government and his colleagues. He eventually had the responsibility of training. My dad eventually received another promotion.

To my five year old self it was becoming clear why my dad was studying at the foot of my bunkbed each night. I knew when he turned the desk lamp off, and it was late. I was resting but not asleep, and this was not good for my schooling the next day.

In 1953, my dad was sent back to Foxboro Instruments to study the principle of maintenance of Foxboro Instruments. He was one of nineteen chosen for this training and again, my dad was the only Negro. He again experienced prejudice while in Boston; none of the white men wanted to share a room with him. The director of the program moved my dad to his daughter's bedroom again, a private home, the bedroom which had a private bath. He felt he got the better deal because the white men had to share a common bathroom.

In 1954, he was sent to California to study at Beckman Instruments; and in 1955, he was sent to Taylor Instruments to continue learning how to operate and maintain the Army Chemical Center's developing automated chemical systems. With the tremendous advances in technology, De Forest Training, Foxboro Instruments, the Bristol Company, Beckman Instruments, and Taylor Instruments were required to move along with the changing landscape of electronics and now no longer existed in their former platforms.

There was a woman who resided in our community, a Catholic, who flirted publicly with my father. I was much too young to know of these types of things, but children are not as unlearned as adults sometimes think. Being so young, I should not have been in an adult environment anyway, but I liked the presence of adults and almost never children. I felt safe around adults; children could be very cruel, and I had not learned any childhood defenses for being so stuck to my mother.

I heard the older folk say, "All good-byes are not gone, and all shut eyes are not sleep!" I was one of those children who heard everything and remembered it too. This female who was interested in my father eventually moved to New York City. When she returned to Edgewood to visit her family, she continued to make public advances on my father. The fact that she was Catholic made her flirtations somehow acceptable to my dad. They had, at the very least, Catholicism in common.

Against my dad's wishes, my mother passed the typing test and was offered a job as clerk typist at the chemical center where my dad was also employed. My dad was furious. The neighborhood men added fuel to their marriage fire by telling my dad that soon my mother would think she was wearing the pants in the house. Women get more mouth when they have money of their own. Keep them barefoot and pregnant, and you can always keep control. This was their advice to my dad. They were idiots!

Although they were both going to the Chemical Center, my dad would not give my mother a ride to work in the mornings. He made her catch the bus. The consequences of not obeying my dad's wishes were harsh, cruel, and severe. He was listening to ignorant men neighbors. It was so out of character for my dad to conduct himself this way. My dad was classical, educated, and intelligent. Being a man was what he wanted to be, so he succumbed to peer pressure of ignorant men.

Of Time and Spirit

I thought my dad's actions were the meanest I had ever seen. He was as stern as a Catholic nun. His not giving her a ride did not deter her. He did not know what my mother was made of, but she showed him. She caught the bus every morning and went to work without complaint. Her attitude was if he wanted to put his ass on his back, then so be it. It hurt me as a child to watch this scenario between my mother and my father. It affected my concentration in elementary school, and I was not the brightest star in the firmament from the start.

Needless to say, I sympathized with my mother and met her every afternoon at the bus stop at the top of the hill that surrounded the gulch setting where we lived. When she returned from work five days per week, I greeted her. My mother and I would talk as I walked her home. I think she was happy to have an ally although I was just a child and had no bearing on the situation.

There was a ghostlike tension in the house between my parents that spilled over onto the children. My mother was aware that men liked to keep women subservient. She was hell-bent and determined it was not going to be her. Further, she did not like women who broke the female code, nor did she like that my dad took no action in turning away. My mother's feelings and emotions were unassailable and resolute. She fought for her rights as a woman and a human being. Slavery was over, and she was emancipated. I observed and learned determination at this intersection of my parents' marital wills. She was the victor. It was a gift to me in the long run to witness this interaction between two people from differing camps of thinking. I learned to never let someone deter me from my higher aims. I am grateful to this day.

Once the army integrated and my dad's salary had increased, we moved to integrated housing on military property, formerly an all-white community. The surrounding county continued not to offer integrated housing. Our new address was 129-F Hawthorne Drive, Edgewood, Maryland. The name of the street sounded so much better to me than 20 Battle Street, a little less militaristic and a little more elevated. I had no idea as a child that the "F" in our address indicated we were still living in an apartment. Hawthorne Drive alongside Battle Street—there was no comparison in accommodations. Hawthorne Drive was far superior. The rooms were twice the size, the kitchen was fully equipped—new stove, refrigerator, white knobless metal wall and floor cabinets—and the bathroom had ceramic tiles and a bathtub. It was spectacular to me,

51

and I was so happy and proud to live there. Number 20 Battle Street was substandard by comparison and had no bathtub, just a shower stall. The shower stall was a dark army-green, five feet by five feet square, a scary site to enter before and after the shower curtain was pulled to enclose you. There was a tin tub for a bath, it was clean but disgusting looking to me.

Previously, we had none of these new features and modern conveniences in our home. Our relatively new Tappan Range and Frigidaire refrigerator were stored in the storage locker provided. I liked that I no longer had to climb to the upper bunkbeds I shared with my brother and my father's workstation. Both beds were now on the floor. It was still an apartment, but as a child, I thought we were living large and moving up.

My mother did not know where we were living on the day we moved to Hawthorne Drive. I met her, as usual, at the bus stop at the top of the hill. I walked her through the forested woods that separated segregated housing to our new apartment in the integrated community. I will never forget she was wearing high-heeled shoes as we walked through the woods that bordered the Negro and now-integrated community, and one of her beautiful shirtwaist dresses. My mother was the fashion plate she wanted to be now that she had a job.

My mother had campaigned for home ownership in Baltimore's Morgan Park. She did not want another apartment. The rent was $90 per month. Ninety dollars a month was big money in 1955 for our family. She thought this money could be going into home ownership versus giving it to the landlord, but my dad refused to buy a house, and so my mother had to settle. I kept my mouth shut but agreed with my mother, really, but what say did I have in the decision?

What my mother did not know at the time was that my dad wanted to be appreciated for what he was providing for his family. He was working and studying to get ahead. In his opinion, my mother was not satisfied and grateful for what he had accomplished. He did not like her attitude. My mother was willing to help buy the house and was anxiously looking ahead to the future. My dad did not want the help of his wife and in no way be dependent on a woman. There was tension in the house again. My mother had begged, but it was to no avail. My dad's masculinity was at stake, in his head.

The community was mixed with many races and cultures. I learned cultural diversity decades before it became popular. The soldiers brought home wives and children from overseas, now what we call mixed-race

Of Time and Spirit

children. In my generation, if you had a drop of Negro blood, you were Negro. Hawthorne Drive was culturally diverse; Battle Street was not. The shortcoming was that I had passed my formative years to actually get the most out of the culturally diverse experience. My dad moved us up to improved housing whereas many Negros remained on Battle Street—some because they could not afford the rent and others because they did not want to be integrated; they instead wanted equality. They did not care to live around or near white people. Some of their experiences and circumstances were more dire than ours.

During this stage, I was in third grade, and I recall my dad ordering for me *Weekly Reader* along with classical music for my childhood record player. *Weekly Reader* was an educational classroom magazine designed for children. It came in the mail each week in my name. I was ecstatic to get mail in my name as a young child and subsequently got interested in ordering things in the mail. *Weekly Reader* was designed for children and covered curriculum themes in the younger grade levels: news-based and current events. In 2012, *Weekly Reader* ceased operations as an independent publication and merged with *Scholastic News*.

Also during this time, I recall playing the small 45 RPM records over and over again, learning the words to every song, but with *Weekly Reader*, I did not cultivate an interest in reading until much later in my life. I have my dad to thank for that. My mother and my dad would order things for me, but they never spent any time with me to learn, become familiar with new things. They were busy keeping a roof over my head; I had to learn to do the rest.

On my own, I boarded the army bus to go to the movies on Saturday afternoons and church on Sunday mornings. I boarded the bus to go to eight o'clock Mass at the Post Chapel. I also went to confession on Saturdays to be prepared for communion on Sunday morning. I occupied and managed my little life as best I could. The army buses were always punctual, and there was no question about safety where I lived. As I got older, I was allowed to go to the six o'clock movies on Saturdays and get back just in time for bed to attend church on Sunday. I had to learn to occupy myself often in my youth. This practice eventually turned into a gift.

In 1957, General Motors, I think, made their most beautiful automobiles. Our neighbors were purchasing the new Chevys and Fords. One soldier purchased a white Lincoln Continental, and the local pharmacist owned

53

a white Cadillac. I hoped my dad would trade in his used 1951 Chevy for a new 1957. Instead, my dad purchased a used 1956 Chevy. He was not the type to compete. He thought we had the new apartment, and that was enough. We did not need a new apartment and a new car to keep up with the Joneses. "Cars depreciate just as soon as you drive them off the showroom floor," he would say. However, the 1956 Chevy turned out to be just as expensive as a new car. It was a lemon.

In 1957, the Army Chemical Center sent my dad back to Foxboro, Massachusetts, to study advanced principles of maintenance, and this assignment was followed by another promotion. There were seventeen men chosen for this class, and my dad was the only Negro. In a photograph I own, I thought he was the most well-groomed and best dressed of all of the men.

My mother was so proud of my dad's accomplishments; and I, of course, liked whatever my mother liked. I was always safe with her. When he went away on these temporary duty assignments, my mother would literally shop for new clothing for the two of us just to take my dad to Friendship Airport to catch the airplane. She and I were not traveling anywhere, but I must say, it we appeared we were. Those were the days when passengers were fashionably dressed to board an airplane.

She would wear an avocado-green wool suit, with matching black patent leather high-heeled shoes and matching handbag. She wore white gloves, small gold-plated button earrings, and was fragrant of Chanel No. 5. Her face was powdered and rouged. She dressed me in the standard navy-blue blazer, gray slacks, white shirt, black dress shoes, and clip-on necktie. We were so proud of my dad. I loved being in the airport; it was so huge compared to any building I had ever been in even the small hangar on the post. It was immaculate and airy. My dad's work brought prestige to our family. He purchased a new Samsonite suitcase and new clothes for his trips; for the most part, he was nonchalant. He was once again being brave and tolerant by going into environments where he was not welcome because of the color of his skin.

My dad was extremely devoted to his mother and his father. We visited my grandmother and my grandfather almost every weekend. When I was young, he brought the whole family to visit. As my brother and my sister got older and moved away from home, it was just the three of us—my father, my mother, and me. He always spent several hours sitting around the kitchen table talking about news and sports. I was bored. My dad's mother and father always kept on hand a case of National Bohemian Beer under their kitchen sink. They would have a beer and talk. I was to be seen but not heard. My vocal privileges were cut short when my dad was around. My mother and I talked incessantly in his absence.

During the summer months, my grandmother would make my mother and my father a mint julip with the fresh mint she grew in her backyard. Alcohol consumption in the Catholic Church was acceptable. I was offered a freshly baked bun from the Lexington Market, Utz Potato Chips, and Minute Maid Orange Juice. I loved these snacks. My mother never purchased fresh-baked buns, potato chips, or ready-made orange juice for the family. She baked her own buns, purchased oranges, and never purchased potato chips. Of course, after I consumed the snacks that my grandmother provided, I was bored again. These visits were considered a family outing; a vacation was unheard of in our family. My dad had a need for his mother too, similar to me and my mother. I always thought he was seeking her acceptance. She was very proud of my dad, but in the most stoic and terse manner, as my dad was to me.

Weekends were not the only time that my dad visited his mother and his father. His parents were the patriarch and the matriarch of the family. They hosted all the six remaining children, their spouses, and the grandchildren for every holiday of the year.

My grandmother hosted the family New Year's Eve party at her house every year with family and friends, serving hot black-eyed peas, a whole ham, cornbread, and enough food for an army. The adults talked, drank, and danced. They sang: "Auld Lang Syne." The family partied until late. It was the only time of the year that I could stay up late.

Every Memorial Day, Fourth of July, and Labor Day, my grandmother's sons pitched in to purchase several dozens of hard-shell Maryland crab, fresh from the Chesapeake Bay. My grandfather had several cases of beer delivered, and the entire family sat around the dining room table eating crabs until their mouths and fingers burned from the Old Bay Seasoning. This was our summer vacation. Everyone was congenial and contented with this arrangement. There was little money for anything else, and Jim Crow laws were in effect, making it unsafe to travel too far during the national holidays. The family was happy to see each other and to get caught up on work, children, play, and gossip too. The women compared their sporty new summer fashions.

In the fall and early winter, we were back at my grandmother's house for Thanksgiving and Christmas dinners. Leaves were placed in the dining room table. The candy jars were full of colorful hard candies, the nut bowls were filled to the brim with salted mixed nuts, while another bowl held hard-shell nuts. My sister and I liked the hard-shell nuts. We left the cracked shells in the bowl. We were later chastised.

The rectangular oak dining table and sideboard buffet was loaded with food: the largest turkeys I had ever seen, white potatoes, gravy, dressing, green beans, hot bread, and dessert. There were no place cards or crystal, but my grandmother always used her Edward M. Knowles wedding china. Knowles started as a pottery company in Chester, West Virginia, during the 1900s. Knowles made dinnerware until the 1930s. I have what is left from the set that is over one hundred years old. I think my grandmother's china was the only luxury item she had in her home, but like everything in her home, she used it frequently. Nothing was saved for special occasions. Everyone pulled up a chair somewhere around the table and ate until they nearly popped. To accommodate everyone, medal folding card table chairs with blue vinyl seats were used in addition to the heaviest upholstered dining chairs ever. It would have been easy to get a hernia pulling those chairs. I always sat next to my mother, never my father.

The adults told old Baltimore family stories of "Once upon a time" and "Do you remember?" I was more-less out of the conversation because I was child and did not know of these early family history stories. It was a lonely time for me since there were no other cousins my age. My mother would say to me: "Poor child! You are too old to be a baby and too young to an adult." The words were of no comfort to me but I endured idle time. Some of those old family stories are the ingredients for this book.

My dad would interject stories of the happenings of where we lived in Edgewood; Edgewood Arsenal where he worked; the coldness of the segregated Post Chapel; and his golfing buddy Logan Johnson and his wife, who were sometimes invited to the New Year's Eve parties.

With an active family and social life, my dad maintained a strong work ethic. He never skipped work or dodged a job. He never called in sick or missed a day. He could build or construct almost anything. Although he was not a college graduate, he made up for his lost education, partaking in all types of upward mobility training courses as a substitute for his lack of a college degree. In many ways, his Catholic school education and Baltimore

City public school education was considered adequate education during his era. He wanted more in life.

My dad's subconscious, held thoughts of losing his opportunity to attend the St. Emma's Military Academy and being turned down twice for Officer's Candidate School. He also carried pain in his heart from the death of his baby sister and his staunch belief in man-made Catholic Church laws that had left him conflicted. Through these life experiences, he worked and maintained an upward professional trajectory. He was driven to do more, someday, somehow, somewhere.

Grade levels and salaries in the federal government are public information. With my dad's increased salary, women stepped up their flirtations. There was a brazen married woman who lived in our community. She was the sister of one of my dad's golf associates. Her husband had an overseas assignment. They had no children. It was rumored that she trapped her husband into marriage to receive his military benefits but did not love him.

Early one Saturday morning, she knocked on the door of our apartment and asked to see my dad. She was of medium height, with chopped-off red-brown hair, possessed a very flat face, and was of very fair complexion. Fair skin for some in the Negro community was commodity. I think she thought her complexion substituted for beauty. She was not beautiful. What I remember most about her attire was her white sleeveless blouse, heavily starched, her everyday bra with the straps visible at the shoulder and armpit, her breasts were as sharply pointed as the head of an arrow. She had on white short shorts. She nervously licked her tongue across her lips, I guess to make them look succulent. She looked like she had had a shower and smelled of cheap powder and lotion. Nothing as high quality as the Chanel my mother wore.

At the time, my mother was standing at the ironing board ironing, in particular, my dad's underwear. My mother opened the door, greeted the woman, and asked her to come into our house. My mother did not ask her to have a seat. After the woman entered, my mother summoned my dad. In a short period, my dad appeared in the living room where the women stood, and in a few moments, the brazen woman and my dad lefttogether. I was aghast.

My mother said nothing. She continued to iron, but soon after, tears fell from her eyes. I had no way of knowing what was transpiring between my dad and the woman, nor of what was transpiring between my mother and my dad, but my mother's tears indicated to me it was not acceptable to her; and if it was not acceptable to her, it was not acceptable to me. More important to me was that I had no way of consoling my mother. It was painful for me to watch as a child. I went to my bedroom and cried for my mother, alone. There was nothing I could do. There was nothing my mother wanted me to do. She always said to me, "I can take care of myself." Nevertheless, I had compassion for my mother.

My dad's staunch and righteous Catholic beliefs had begun to subside after serving in the military. He was mocked by other soldiers for his strong and righteous convictions and beliefs in Catholicism while serving in the army. He was challenged by others who did not believe as he believed. He was shocked by himself that he did not have sound explanations to provide to his fellow soldiers for what he believed. The military machoism had an effect on my dad.

When he learned to question his Catholic beliefs and did not find reasonable explanations from the church, he slowly became less enchanted with the Catholic Church. Thus when his children were of age, he did not insist that we believe all the things he had believed about Catholicism in his childhood.

My sister was the most academically astute of my parent's three children. My mother implored that my dad let her go to Saint Frances Academy for Girls as my dad's sisters had. My dad refused. My mother could discern that my sister had the abilities of my father. She wanted my sister to have, as a female, the same solid education that he had gotten. It would have been a better education than she was receiving at the one-room school in the neighboring enclave. His answer remained, no!

My mother saw the value of the Catholic Schools in the primary grades. She also thought all children needed some spiritual enrichment early in their life. If the child wanted to change religions in adulthood, that would be their decision. My dad insisted, "No, it just messes you up." This was his new thinking. He felt crippled by his Catholic indoctrination. Some of the soldiers' influences made my dad feel foolish.

In this situation, my sister lost an opportunity to attend Saint Frances, just as my dad lost an opportunity at Saint Emma's, but for different reasons. My dad had no vision for my sister's future success in life because he was still struggling to figure out his life. Further, he did not think girls needed to be smart. He was a chauvinist. He was resistant. His decision and state of mind for my sister did not endear him to me. I was happier being attached to my mother.

I believe my dad was obsessed and confused in his attempts to apply his religion's teachings to his life experiences as a soldier and as a civilian in the world. I was shocked to learn that my dad was so naïve about Catholicism. I was baptized, attended summer Bible classes, confirmed. I regularly went to confession and took Holy Communion in the Catholic Church. I never believed the Catholic teachings as wholeheartedly as my dad. Maybe my public school education was not so bad after all. What was solid and clear is that both my mother and my father and their respective parents were go-to-church Christians: Catholic, Presbyterian, and Methodist; but from my young eyes and my Sunday school teachings, Christianity had its problems of interpretation from my perspective.

My dad would reluctantly attend church at my mother's request for the sake of the children. He also felt an intense obligation to his mother, a devout Catholic, and the church to raise his children Catholic. Even as an adult, he was tangled up in his head with the Catholic Church and their teachings. He wrote in his notes that he resented man-made church laws of any church.

With his three children, my dad was a disciplinarian when necessary. In short, he expected obedience at all times. He was extremely fair. He attempted reasoning with his children first. He never used physical force, but he got his message across. You obeyed, or there were consequences, definitely of the Catholic school type, if not downright militaristic. My dad knew how to interrogate and melt you down.

He never raised his voice to my mother or his children. He never used profanity of any kind. He did not talk much and never of sex. He ensured that there was milk and bread in the house. He believed in good shoes for all of us. He had perfectly neat feet except for chronic athlete's feet he picked up in the army. He never could get rid of it, and all of us had to bleach the tub or shower floor after his use.

As we got older, he told all of us that he wanted to "break a plate." This was an anthem almost every day if someone was out of line. The unspoken implication was that we were to grow up and move out of his house. He did not teach dependence. He believed everyone should learn to take care of themselves. If everyone could do this, then there would be no need for welfare. Neither he nor his father believed in public welfare or accepted it.

He provided us with two options: the first was going to college and the second going in the military for the boys and getting married for my sister. However, if you did not choose one of those two options and stayed at home, you paid rent and still followed his rules. His rules were rigid. He was fair and reasonable with the rent. In any event, the free ride for his children would be over at age 18 was his message to us. Underneath of it all, I think he tired of raising children and struggling to find himself too.

He also reiterated, "When you leave home make sure you are completely prepared because once you leave you can't come back." If he got talk back from his children, he would say, "I won't ask you for anything and don't you ask me for anything." He was tough, but all he really required was obedience. Being the youngest, I learned from my brother and sister's mistakes. I learned obedience and how to soften my dad too. I got everything I ever wanted from him but never asked for much. He knew I was brown-nosing him, and it pained him, but I could at times weaken his defenses. He spoiled me too. He would say to me, "You think you are a privileged charter." I lived at home the longest, and my dad did not want me to leave—he encouraged me to stay longer. I learned how to work with my dad, and I grinned when I knew I had gotten over.

I believe if my dad's children seriously needed to stay at home, he would have allowed it; but he repeated his anthem so much I think all of us were glad to leave home. He forced us to spread our wings and make our own lives, mistakes, and triumphs.

CHAPTER 6

Father Culture

1955

My dad gave our apartments and home a high-end classical tone with the music that played in the background of our lives. He was indeed a cultured man. He continued to play music of all types.

Over and over, we continued to hear the classics of Ludwig van Beethoven, Franz Liszt, Franz Joseph Haydn, Franz Joseph, and Richard Wagner. Prelude to Act 1, *Tristan Und Isolde*; "Tannhauser Overture," Pyotr Illyich Tchaikovsky's *Symphony #6 in B minor Pathetique, Scheherazade* by Nikolai Rimsky-Korsakov, and other world-class music and musicians.

Swan Lake and the *Nutcracker Suite* were the first pieces of classical musical he taught me. I used to call The Nutcracker Suite, The Nutcracker Suit, and my dad would laugh at me. "It's *suite*, knucklehead!" he would giggle and say to me.

He liked the big band sounds of Duke Ellington, Count Basie, Stan Getz, Tommy Dorsey, and Artie Shaw. He liked popular artists like Roy Hamilton, Sarah Vaughn, and, especially, Ella Fitzgerald singing in Ella in Berlin *Mack the Knife*. He got a kick out of Sammy Davis and Carmen McRae singing "Baby It's Cold Outside." He loved the Lionel Hampton recording *Silver Vibes*.

He enjoyed the Broadway plays *My Fair Lady, The King and I, Kismet, The Sound of Music, Purlie, Porgy and Bess,* and the lover's duet, *Manhattan Tower*. My brother called Porgy and Bess, Porgy and Bessie to be funny. All the children were entertained and learned to love the music my dad loved. He would say to us, "My dad played classical music for us. We would all sit around the radio and listen to good music as children." My dad's love of music was passed down from his father. My dad's music was the only thing my siblings and I had in common.

I actually envisioned and learned tremendously from my dad's choices of music. *Manhattan Tower* was written by Gordon Jenkins in the 1940s. It is the story of a young man who travels to New York City for a visit and had a brief love affair. The description of New York City in "Magical City," New York's My Home, *Married I Can Always Get*, and *The Statue of Liberty* were all selections that served as my inspiration to visit New York City from a very early age. From the music, I made it a point to visit New York City, and I made my first solo trip to after college byway of a Greyhound Bus. I saw the play *Pippin*. I have continued to love New York since my first visit many years ago.

My Fair Lady, starring Rex Harrison and Julie Andrews, was a hit in our house too. My dad liked the selections "Why Can't the English?" and "With a Little Bit of Luck." I liked the selection "Without You," for this selection reminded me of my mother, a strong woman who learns to assert herself and to stand up to a man. Considering I was timid and voiceless, I found my voice from assertive women.

The assertive theme replayed itself in *The King and I*, when Mrs. Anna speaks up to the King Mongkut of Siam. This was an American musical with the film stars Deborah Kerr and Yul Brynner. Yul Brynner and Clark Gable were the two only men I ever saw my mother admire. My dad was unthreatened by her comments; he would jokingly remark under his breathe to me, "I wish they would take her!" The investment in wardrobe for Broadway musicals then pale in comparison to many of those today. My dad and I converged on the song "A Puzzlement." We both thought the lyrics were reflective of a changing world.

The King of Siam struggles to explain to Mrs. Anna and himself why leadership of his people was so confusing and difficult. He introduces this song when he was a boy and concludes the song as a man questioning why the rules of a king need to change, but learns the world is changing around him, and Mrs. Anna brings this to his attention.

My dad and I converged on this song because we both agreed the world changes, and it is difficult to remain of the same opinion forever because the world is constantly changing. We both agreed with King

Of Time and Spirit

Mongkut—it is a puzzlement. My dad and I also learned that we needed to change toward each other. The thinking of his childhood experiences did not apply to my childhood experience, and I needed to consider why he felt to me the way he did. We both needed to recalibrate our attitudes toward each other. *The King and I* was good for us.

And finally, on topic of music, every Saturday morning, my dad played *The Sound of Music* by Richard Rogers with lyrics by Oscar Hammerstein II. This musical was based on the memoir *The Story of the Trapp Family Singers*. I learned of Austria and the loss of their homeland to the Nazis. So much of what I learned from my dad's music was not taught in the segregated primary school I attended. My dad's music was another absolute gift to me. This proves that all learning does not take place in a school.

My dad was a stickler about his records, both 45s and 33 1/3 RPMs. He had an RCA Victor record player for his 45 RPMs. When 33 1/3's became popular, he purchased a console blond wood cabinet with a turntable and room for storage inside the cabinet for what he called the long plays. My mother hated the cabinet because it did not match her mahogany furniture. He wiped the dust from each record before playing them. He used a soft toothbrush to clean "his" diamond sapphire needle. He liked perfect sound. He was proud of owning this stuff. Music excited him.

His sound system and records were a few of his adult toys. He did not want the children playing around with his musical equipment. He would actually hide his 45 RPM record player so that my brother would not get tempted to play it in his absence. He knew that my brother would not follow his directions. When my brother took the risk of playing my dad's record player, when he lifted the lid, there would be a note inside, "Roswell, put me back!" This was a lifetime family joke. The children had an old Philco record player and radio to play their 1950s rock 'n' roll music.

He purchased children's classics for me to listen to on my children's record player. My dad was very protective of his library of music. Nobody was to touch it, but when he played his music, we had a classy home, and we all gathered for music appreciation classes held by my dad.

My dad was an avid reader and enjoyed literature of all types. His favorite book was *The Razor's Edge* by W. Somerset Maugham (1874–1965). I do not know when this book descended into to his life. It was published in 1944. This book became my dad's bible. He lived and preached this book. He loved the main character, whose name was Larry Darrell, an American pilot traumatized by his experiences in World War I. He set off on a path to search for the meaning of his life. Larry traveled to the Himalayas to understand civilization. My dad could identify with Larry because he too was trying to understand the meaning of his life. My dad was this type of seeker. Larry and my dad rejected conventional life and searched for meaningful experiences in a materialistic world.

When I was a teen, my dad gave me *The Razor's Edge* to read. After I finished reading the book he asked me, "Who is your favorite character?" He so much wanted me to like the book and get from the book what he had gotten from his reading of it, and, most of all, love and admire Larry Darrell's life quest. When I announced that I loved Elliott Templeton, my dad said, "No! Elliott was a materialistic snob! You were supposed to like Larry. You didn't get it!" He was disgusted with me because I chose Elliott as my favorite character. I liked Elliott because he was savvy. In addition to having in-resident staff, including a chef and valet, Elliott was the type of man who had a personal barber, tailor, and masseurs to fight the ravages of time. Elliott hosted grand parties and sent invitations that were embossed and engraved. I was totally thrilled that Elliott even had custom-made silk pajamas and underwear engraved with his initials, whereas my dad was shocked that I could be so taken by such fanfare.

When the Great Depression occurred and all of Elliott's hoity-toity friends laughed and made fun of his weddedness to society and materialism, Elliott had sense enough to move his wealth to conservative funds, thus never losing a cent of his money as most others had. When he was asked how he had managed to have money when almost everyone lost money, Elliott simply replied to friends who had subbed him and underestimated his ability to be a substantial person, as my dad had done me, "God tempers the wind to the shorn lamb!" Elliott, though ridiculed, showed his mettle at a time of desperation for most others. This is where I identified with Elliott.

My dad believed Elliott to be a fool. He wanted me to like Larry who represented the essence of the book and man's quest for spiritual peace but moreover who my dad identified and too was on the same quest. Instead, I chose the worldly, high born, well-bred, refined gentleman of high society. My dad just shook his head. He said to me: "I am just wasting my time on you boy!" I thought the character Larry was as naïve and as crazy as my dad, running to the Himalayas looking for inner peace. Peace is inside of you not the Himalayas. His favorite book was another example of how

Of Time and Spirit

much my dad and I were not on the same page. This was similar to our differences between *Tannhauser* and *La Cage aux Follies*.

I thought I was entitled to like whichever character I liked, not who he wanted me to like. Elliott Templeton was a character in a fiction book, not a real-life person. This was my dad's and my relationship at this stage of the game, but I still read and own his original copy of *The Razor Edge* and read it every ten years as he did, and I still like Elliott Templeton as my favorite character—and by the way Elliott was Catholic; maybe this book was recommended by the nuns in Catholic school. Biblically, it is said, *The sharp edge of a razor is difficult to pass over; thus the wise say the path to Salvation is hard.*

The manner of very high elegance in which W. Somerset Maugham described his male characters made me think that he was gay. When I did research on him in *Wikipedia*, I found that he had been described as bisexual—having relationships with women, marriage, and children in his early years, and ending his life with two successful relationships with men.

My dad's face was always in a book or newspapers. He often checked out books from the main branch of the Enoch Pratt Free Library as he did as a child. He enjoyed the library. As a family, we drove past the Central Branch at 400 Cathedral Street as we traveled US Route 40 westbound on Franklin Street heading to my grandmother and grandfather's house at 1832 West Franklin Street. We would see the library again when we rode US Route 40 eastbound on West Mulberry Street returning home.

My dad took me there once or twice, but I thought the central hall was dark, old, moldy, dusty, and musty during the 1950s. It was established in 1882 and eventually expanded to Cathedral Street, occupying three-quarters of a block. There were old hard oak wood chairs, dim lights, and stale air. The men's bathroom smelled foul, and men loitered there. At that point in my life, I had no interest in locating books for I had not yet developed an interest in books. The public school library I attended was smaller and reachable. The school library had more books than I would ever read, which was not much. I was not a reader compared to him, but he was an excellent role model for my adult years, mainly after college. My dad and my sister were the family intellectuals and my inspiration and introduction to reading. I include my late partner to this list as well.

My dad could make almost anything from scratch. I asked him to build me a bookcase since my bedroom was larger and I wanted a place to display my personal things. He built me a bookcase, stained and lacquered it for me. It was a three-tier arrangement, somewhat rustic and homemade looking. I loved the bookcase and seem to arrange and rearrange my little life there each day. The bookcase was a calming balm in a weird way. I could make my own sense of order. I learned that I loved organization in my life on this bookcase.

My dad loved the art work of Paul Gauguin. W. Somerset Maugham wrote a book capturing the life of Paul Gauguin in his novel *The Moon and Sixpence*. My dad also gave me this book to read, and I thoroughly enjoyed it as well as *The Razor's Edge*. My dad was a regular at the museums and had a great appreciation for many artists; however, Paul Gauguin painted Polynesian subjects in brown colors that my dad could appreciate and identify with. My dad visited art museums in France, Italy, and Germany while in the army. The subjects in European art were mostly white, including Jesus Christ, who was a man of color. My dad liked the fact that Paul Gauguin left France to escape civilization, as character Larry in *The Razor's Edge* did, to paint the scenes seizing the local Tahitian life experiences.

It always annoyed me when my dad said he wanted to live on an island like Paul Gauguin and escape civilization. I felt he wanted to desert my mother and his family. He sounded crazy to me. He was doing very well in my eyes, his family was living well, why would he want to live on an island? It did not sound normal to me, but I was a child. Paul Gauguin left his wife and six children in France, had multiple children in Tahiti, and died of syphilis. I am not sure whether my dad knew of or liked that part of Gauguin's life. My dad disliked hoity-toity people. "They called themselves civilized . . . and their French airs, are a crock of . . .," my dad would say.

My dad was a great ballroom dancer. On the occasional Saturday evenings, my dad and my mother went out on the town, and they danced together before leaving home to his favorite big band music. One Saturday evening, they danced to the full rendition of Ella Fitzgerald singing in 1960 Ella in Berlin Mack the Knife. The lyrics to this day resonate in my mind. Ella, a jazz singer, introduced as the only woman to have ever sung this song. She speaks to the audience, who are wild about her singing and the preceding songs she sung at the live concert. After thunderous applause, she gets serious and launches into the song.

Ella sings the song with such passionate verve, sparkle, vitality; but mid-song, she forgets the original lyrics, thus she improvises with zest and words that rhyme. She sings and swings the song along with her band

Of Time and Spirit

to an uproarious loving and accepting crowd. The crowd loves her as she closes the song, singing with laughter, amazed that she was able to pull the improvisation off with such resounding success.

Ella's audience goes wild. My parents dance through the whole selection. This album of *Ella in Berlin* was inducted into the Grammy Hall of Fame in 1999, which is a special Grammy award established in 1973 to honor recordings that are at least twenty-five years old, and that have "qualitative or historical significance." Ella received the Best Female Vocal Performance in a single and vocal performance, female album at the Third Annual Grammy Awards.

My mother knew how to dress elegantly; she did not look like a dowdy housewife or matronly like some of the military wives. Fashion was often her weapon to ward off other women. She could upstage most women with her high-quality fashions choices. She sometimes wore a scarlet red wool dress, with a flared skirt with a thin natural leopard belt, with gold tooling. She wore black high-heeded shoes and her thick, shiny black hair crowned her. I thought she looked stunning. It was my favorite of her fancy dresses and accessories. My parents danced in our rather large living room, an area of the floor that was covered with a green wool 9X12 carpet. My mother purchased our home furnishings. My mother preferred the period style of Duncan Phyfe—styles that she was familiar with from her native hometown of Washington DC. She always said the family was dancing holes in her good wool carpet. My sister and I would dance too. We all continued to dance on the green wool carpet until it was no more.

My dad would sometimes chastise my mother for trying to lead him on the dance floor. It frustrated him. He would chide her, "Zelma!" My mother had energy and was very much into appearances and cared more about how good they appeared on the dance floor versus the accuracy of the steps. My dad was a systems man; he did things properly and precisely, but slow!

I thought they were a nice-looking couple, and I liked to see them dance. Dance was the only thing I ever saw them do that appeared affectionate. I never saw them hug or kiss. I hated to see them leave the house on Saturday nights because I hated being home alone with my older brother.

Each of my dad's classical interests stands out to me because I was raised in rural segregated housing and I attended segregated schools. I did not hear or see any of my dad's cultural passions and life interest in

67

the community where I lived. Many of the men in my community were loud, drinkers, abusers, hunters, fishermen, fighters, and womanizers. My dad's urban social class distinguished him from my rural segregated environment. My dad's difference is my inspiration for writing this book; he was an unusual man to me. Most of my schoolteachers were college educated; however, my exposure to my dad made me stand out as a student. I was a misfit in the setting I was raised. He was a misfit too, but this was where he worked, made his home, and raised his children. He made this part of his life's work.

From my earliest memories, my dad had a lifelong sense of humor. Everything was funny; he found humor in all aspects of life. He told jokes all the time and would laugh until tears fell from his eyes and his nose would drip. He needed his handkerchief to dry is eyes and his nose. My brother and my sister seemed to get the punch lines of the jokes he told. They laughed vigorously, thus rewarding and encouraging him to continue with his the laughter and gaiety. I was much younger and struggled to understand my dad's jokes. I regularly didn't get the punch line. They laughed at me because I didn't understand. Rarely, if I did understand the joke, I never found it to be funny. I thought the three of them silly.

"Maurice doesn't get it," he would say. Eventually, I became the butt end of my dad's jokes. That was my penalty for not catching on to his jokes and rewarding his sense of humor. He wanted applause. I never found being laughed at funny, by my dad or my siblings. On most occasions, my mother did not get the joke, or did not find it funny either; but on one occasion, she laughed at me too. My feelings would be hurt. It made me feel my whole family was laughing at me. At times, my self-esteem suffered, but there was no sympathy. You had to grow tough in my family. The lesson, I suppose, was to toughen up; but I always felt a victim inside. At this age, I could not wait to grow up and move out on my own. I wanted to escape my entire family.

My dad told this joke to the family one Saturday morning. Most of my dad's jokes originated from his colleagues at work. He thought the jokes hilarious. He couldn't wait to tell this one:

When the body was first made, all parts wanted to be boss.

The brain said, "Since I control everything and do all the thinking, I should be the boss."

The feet said, "Since I carry man where he wants to go and get him in position to do what the brain wants, I should be the boss."

The hands said, "Since I must do all the work and earn all the money to keep the rest of you going, I should be the boss."

The eyes said, "Since I must look out for all of you and tell you where the danger lurks, I should be boss."

And so, it went with the heart, ears, and lungs, and finally the asshole spoke up and demanded that it should be the boss. All of the other parts laughed and laughed at the idea of the asshole being the boss. The asshole was so angered that he blocked himself off and refused to function.

The lung limply at each side. The heart and lungs struggled to keep going. All pleaded with the brain to relent and let the asshole be the boss; and so, it happened.

All other parts did the work, and the asshole just bossed and passed out a lot of shit.

The moral: You don't have to be a brain to be boss, just an asshole.

As a child, I failed to find the humor in this joke as well. Considering that I was a manager of people later in my career, I still don't fine the humor in this joke. Humor and ridicule is always funny when it is not directed toward you.

I caught a chest cold, and my mother was too tired to get out of bed to give me another dose of cough syrup. She sent my dad to administer the medication, but instead, he gave me two tablespoons of gin. In the morning, my mother would say to my dad, "How much medicine did you give that child? He has not awakened yet?"

My dad would say, "I gave him a couple of tablespoons of gin!" My mother would scold him, but he would reply, "Well, he stopped coughing so we could get some sleep, didn't he!" He thought this kind of thing humorous too. I did not! I thought my dad was juvenile at times.

My dad was a humorist poet too. When he transitioned from the army to long-term domestic living with my mother, he could not understand why my mother had such a hard time getting out of bed in the morning. He was regimented to get up early in the morning, and he went to bed precisely at ten every night, barring none. He could never seem to get her up. He never considered that she was tired from washing clothes, ironing, keeping the house immaculate, cooking meals three times per day, packing he children's lunches, and performing other duties as they cropped up.

My mother loved to sleep, don't get me wrong, but she needed sleep too. She would say, "If God made anything greater than sleep, he kept it for himself." My dad found it tiring, waiting for my mother to get the day started. He awakened early each morning and prepared his breakfast and drank coffee. The newspaper was delivered early each morning, and he would read and enjoy his solitude long before anyone else in the house arose. He often prepared the breakfast for the children, an agreement he and my mother made years earlier. After twenty years of marriage, he wrote this original poem about my mother:

When the clock goes off in the morning
And everyone ceases to snore
There's quite a buzz of activity from everyone
But Zelma wants five minutes more.
How well do I remember, last evening as I turned off the lights
and locked the door?
Zelma said it was too early to retire
She wanted to stay up five minutes more.
I don't give a darn, how hard I try,
It's been twenty years I am sure
Threatening, arguing, scolding it's no good
That woman still wants five minutes more.
When all of our lives are over and done
And Gabriel's horn is heard from shore to shore
Other people will bust from the graves
But you won't see Zel, she is getting five minutes more.

My dad recited this poem to everyone who visited. It was true and clever. My mother was not offended, and my siblings liked it too. I was the oddball. I thought he was making fun of my mother and further squashing her need to even get some rest in her own house. My dad and I were often in different camps in our thinking.

From my dad's military years, he continued to stay in great physical shape. He took great pride in being athletic and fit. He regularly performed sit-ups and push-ups on our famous green pure-wool living room carpet. He could even balance himself on his head. He taught me how to perform these exercises too. I was always amazed at myself when I mastered something like this. If I stuck more with my dad, I could have learned so much more; but we were an odd couple.

My dad played a fair game of golf and continued to enjoy swimming. I took little interest in either sport. In the backyard of the Edgewood Arsenal Post Chapel, he would practice his golf shots. Sometimes he would take me along to hit a few balls. My dad had no patience with me if I did not learn quickly. Time was important to him. He would become impatient with me, and I would become impatient with his impatience with me. This was the case in both swimming and golf. In retrospect, I wish I could have stuck with sports and practiced on my own, but sports never appealed to me.

He subsequently taught me to caddy for him. I learned and preferred to caddy for him than have him teach me to golf. There were too many skills needed to perfect the game of golf. He taught me the difference between the wood and iron clubs, the tees, cleaning the balls, and replacing the sod after teeing off. Most of all, knowing where his ball landed at the other end of the golf course. This I could do. We played nine, eighteen, and, rarely, thirty-six holes of golf. Carrying the clubs was heavy work. I never tired. He paid me top dollar to caddy. I always appreciated his fairness toward me. He never cheated on me or ripped me off just because I was his son and a dependent he felt owed him something.

Rarely, my dad would treat himself to some golf clothes from Hamburger's at One Charles Center in downtown Baltimore. Hamburger's was well known and one of the top men's clothiers at the time. My dad was not a big shopper, but if he ever purchased anything, it was tasteful and of good quality. He looked really classic in his golf attire. This to me was another symbol of my dad's becoming successful because Negros were not playing golf in those day compared to football and other contact sports.

My dad was distinguished, smart, and handsome. He stood out in a rural town like Edgewood. Women from around the neighborhood flirted with him all the time, to the extent I could tell that it was an annoyance to my mother, considering she honored other women and the women's code. Regardless of how close my mother was to my father or me, she stood up for women as a group. It made no difference to some of the women that he was married with children, or that they were in some way in violation of the women's code. They too were married or unmarried, with and without children. Their husbands were overseas or reassigned to another post. Some were rather brazen and ruthless too. As an onlooker, I did not like my mother being disrespected, but she had her own formula for managing these types of women. Whatever her style of managing, she was the winner.

My mother was confident. She was quick to tell my father, "Suit yourself!" Or, "Go ahead, man, shake your business!" Or, "I know how to take care of myself." She was never perturbed or made a scene when it came to other women. My mother was self-assured, and she appeared tempered and to have planned it that way. She was not weak; she knew her position, and these types of women did not linger very long when she made her moves.

A few men were envious of my dad's popularity with women. One hot summer day, a late Saturday morning, a hungover, loudmouth neighbor asked my dad in my presence, "Ros, are you messing around with all these women who seem to like you so much?"

My dad looked at the man and calmly replied, "No!"

The loudmouth neighbor shouted to my dad, "You a got-dam lie!" The man was so loud and vulgar my little body vibrated from the resonance of his voice.

I had never heard my dad use a foul word, nor had I ever heard anyone disrespect him. My dad looked at me and said, "Let's go, Maurice!" And we just walked away. My dad said to me, "When someone approaches you like that, consider the source, make the allowance, and walk away. You don't need to respond to anyone who speaks to you in that manner." Although my dad was calm with me, I knew he was fuming to have been confronted in that manner in front of me. I am sure my dad revisited that comment with our neighbor when I was not present, no doubt about it; and although the man lived next door, I never saw him speak to my dad again.

He would whine behind my dad's back, "The Dorseys think they are better than everyone else."

In 1957, my dad gave me an English Racer Bicycle for my tenth birthday. He did not give many gifts for the children that I was aware, but if you ever got one, it was top shelf. The English Racer was a beautiful bicycle. It had to be the most expensive bike in the neighborhood. I didn't take a lot of interest in it, just like the big blue tricycle he gave me when I was four or five years old. He was trying hard to connect with me, but I was a lapdog-type child. I was coddled and sheltered.

My dad taught me how to ride the bicycle and how to change the gears. It had three speeds, but the chain often got jammed when the gears changed. He appreciated the bicycle and its worthiness and wanted me to as well. I am sure it was something he would like to have had as a child. My mother was annoyed that he bought me a bike because she knew that I would not have sustained interest in it because I was a house child. Further, she did not want me dragging the bike into the house every day across her carpet or risk scratching her mahogany furniture. The apartment did not have a back door—one way in and one way out!

One afternoon after school, I was bringing the bicycle in for the evening; in the process, the screened door slammed really hard, and she shouted, "Stop slamming that door when you come into the house!" I tried to explain that I was struggling to bring in my bicycle. She said, "I don't care if you are bringing in a Mack Truck. Don't slam the door!" As a result, I showed less and less interest in the bicycle since she made it such an unpleasant experience to simply use it. Further, she did not think it made sense to purchase that kind of gift for me anyway. It was eventually disappeared. Stolen. I think.

The greatest gift my dad ever taught me was the meaning of the word *gratitude*. I will never forget I was riding along with him in his used 1956 Chevrolet. He was in a good mood that day, and he decided to stop at the Jewish Bakery of US Route 40 East to purchase for himself some gingerbread. My dad loved gingerbread. While he was making his purchase, he caught me, eyeballing cookies shaped like gingerbread boys topped with icing for the eyes, nose, and mouth, and topping bordered his hands and feet. I had never seen such a beautiful cookie.

I never asked my dad for anything, but he saw how enchanted I was with the little cookies. They were terribly expensive, I thought, for a cookie. He asked, "Would you like to have one?"

I replied, "Can I have two?" Had I been with my mother, she would have gotten me a half dozen; therefore I did not think asking for two was too much.

He sternly replied, "No! I only asked you if you wanted one. You can take the one, or you get nothing. which do you chose?" He was so stern with me that it took all the pleasure out of having the cookie. I wanted to tell him that I didn't want any because he was so nasty; however, I accepted the one, but my feelings were hurt because I didn't think he needed to be so harsh. My dad could be cold. He was worse than the Catholic nuns that taught him. It came from his mother's side of the family.

When we got in the car to continue with the ride home, I had my one cookie sitting in my lap. It was so expensive they packaged it in a small box with a ribbon. I pouted. His sharpness got to me. He saw that I had lost my childhood glow. He said, "Maurice, you must learn to be grateful for what you have. People are not required to give you anything."

I was a child, and it took practice over the years of my life to learn gratefulness, but my dad's scolding was a lifelong gift to me. I cry, however, when I relive the memory of this lesson. I still think he was too harsh and could have handled the situation differently. With all of his sophistication, he could be a little rough around the edges at times, if not downright militaristic.

I recognized in my childhood that my dad had aspirations of moving up in the world and finding his place. He had a solid education, and although he came from poor beginnings, he was a very classy man. He was always clean, neatly dressed, tall, dark, and handsome. He was almost elegant. I thought that intellectually, he was a cut above his peers and most people I was exposed to. He could handle a great conversation with the elite or the poor.

Both of my parents were working full-time for the government. We had steady income, and both my parents managed money flawlessly well. They created a balanced, stable environment for their children. We always had good food, clothing, and shelter. They both participated in the PTA. My dad got along with our teachers, and especially well with Mr. Robert Paige, the music teacher at the Central Consolidated School. My dad knew of all the music the music teacher taught; however, my dad did not play an instrument. Mr. Paige did play several instruments.

After World War II, Edgewood Arsenal was beginning to have troubles due to the publicity on their testing human subjects with chemicals similar to the Tuskegee Airmen. They slowly began the process of downsizing or shutting down many of their military installations. As a result, civilian personnel were no longer eligible to live in subsidized military housing. Civilian families had to find their own housing. My mother had harped on my dad for years to buy a house. She thought it a waste of money to pay rent when the equity from a house could be used as a cushion to remain independent in old age. She was correct, but my dad still woofed.

In my mother's thinking, she was not depending on her children to take care of her in old age, as many parents did during that generation. She said, "I don't want to live with any of my children." She would say, "Just because you gave birth [to your children], it did not mean they were going to take care of you!" She was adamant in this thinking. My dad thought that incorrect. He would have happily lived with any of his children in old age. The fact is home equity can be a cushion in old age.

My dad was very reluctant to buy a house. He hated the concept of debt, finance charges, and being obligated to any institution. He liked being mentally free. He grew up in an apartment, and that was good enough for him. He was sensible with money—his money and your money too if you were fool enough to bring it up in conversation. You could trust my dad with every penny you owned. He was an honest man right down to the cent.

But this time he had to make a decision. The housing inventory for Negros was limited in Harford County. His options were to move back to Baltimore and commute seventy-five to one hundred miles per day or buy a piece of land and build a house in the county. Regardless of what either one of my parents wanted, they had ninety days to vacate the premises of our current residence.

He chose to buy land and have a house built. This would at least provide for him a shorter commute. The land and the house were cheaper in the county as compared to a house in the city, which translated to less debt. My dad did not like shackles, and that's what a house meant to him. He was the solid character Larry Darrell in *The Razor's Edge* with his thinking here.

He tore a quote from the cartoon section of the newspaper that read,

> *Because, is it not true, as Epicurus once said . . . that wealth consists not of having great possessions . . . but in having few wants?*

My dad lived by this statement. He was never a collector of possessions, and his wants were few. He was like this his whole life. For those like me and my mother, he thought we were idiots for being materialistic.

While the new house was being built, we moved to temporary housing in a small two-bedroom asbestos shingled semidetached rental on 23 Emery Street. By this time, my sister and my brother had left home. My dad had "ha, ha" broken two plates. From my preteen observations, making this transition from apartment to homeownership was very stressful for my dad. He hated the process of building a house, the cost it entailed, and the freedom he had to give up from sport and play to maintain a property. It just went against his grain.

After the contract was signed with the builder, my mother started a shopping spree for home furnishings. She was happy and appeared too careless about my dad's distaste with homeownership. She thought it foolish to pay rent year after year. At last, she was going to have the home she dreamed of owning for years.

My dad and my mother argued frequently over the selection of exterior and interior materials used in the construction of the house. My mother always selected the more expensive materials, and my dad selected the cheapest. My mother wanted an all-brick house with a fireplace; my dad did not. My mother wanted ceramic tiles in the bathroom; my dad wanted molded plastic. Listening to these squabbles was unsettling for me and my concentration in school. I had no skills for tuning them out. I felt in-it.

My dad continued to drank gin, and my mother continued her shopping sprees. It was not a happy time for either of us. I was ignored completely for they were consumed in battle. I did as many household chores as possible to take the pressure off of them and to keep some modicum of peace. I asked few questions, kept quiet, and stayed out of their way. Getting the house completed and getting settled was the topic of most conversations. What was most striking to me in this house was the absence of music. In addition, my dad had no one to laugh at his jokes in that my sister and my brother were gone, and I never found humor in his jokes anyway. There was no *My Fair Lady* from my dad and no Wings Over Jordan Choir or Dinah Washington from my mother.

One of my greatest memories of my father on Emery Street was that he continued his early riser routine. He got up early when the house was quiet. He made his breakfast of two fried eggs cooked in bacon drippings; two slices of bacon; two slices of toast with butter, not margarine; and coffee

Of Time and Spirit

with cream and sugar. He would set the table and fold the tablecloth in half, just for his place setting. He read his newspaper or a book at every meal except dinner with the family. He preferred to eat alone—no noise. This was serenity time for him.

When I came to the table in preparation for school, I felt isolated from him. This was added to my other accumulated childhood slights from him. He would make me breakfast until I learned to make my own, but he never wanted to talk. He wanted quiet, and if I opened my mouth to speak, he would say, "Quiet." If I interrupted him he would repeat "Quiet!" Whatever was going on in him, it was another form of rejection for me. Thus, I ate my breakfast in silence. He and my mother went to work each morning. I caught the school bus to ride fifteen miles to a segregated to school. It was a grim time for me.

My dad's habits were consistently the same with everything. He did everything at the same time every day. It would drive my mother nuts. He even went to the bathroom at the same time every day. He would announce, "Well, I guess I'll go take a dump now." We all knew his pattern; he didn't need to elucidate. He was our breadwinner. It is said, *He who makes the gold, also makes the rules.* My mother and I were pretty much put on Mute under these circumstances. The absence of my brother and my sister surely made a difference in our household for my dad.

At Christmastime, I still wanted a Christmas tree although my sister and my brother had left home. Emery Street was small and cramped. My mother was storing her new purchases for the new house in my bedroom until moving day. My bedroom was full to ceiling level with tables, chairs, lamps, linens, dishes, and other things for the house.

I was entering my teens; neither of my parents were in the mood to deal with me, and they did not see why at twelve years old I still needed a Christmas tree when they were spending so much money on the house. I made a fuss, and my dad reluctantly got me a tree. He did not place it in the stand as he usually did. He just got me a tree and sat it in the corner of the living room. I was charged with setting the tree in the stand for myself. The house looked like a junkshop in preparation for the move, and perhaps I should have skipped the tree; but I needed something for myself to cope with their dysfunction.

I attempted on my own to get the tree in the stand. I was unable to manage the weight of the tree at the base alone, but after significant struggling, I got it in the stand. But it stood lopsided. I couldn't get the tree to stand straight, so I took a string and tied it from the center and nailed the string to the wall with hopes that the tree would stand straight and not topple down. It looked tacky. I placed all the lights and ornaments on the tree anyway. It was not as appealing as when my dad placed it in the stand and my sister and I decorated it together. She was better with tree decorations.

A small group of neighbors arrived at our house for an after-party during the holidays. They were pretty spirited. My dad poured drinks, put on some dance music, and they all started swing dancing. While they danced, they repeatedly hit the Christmas tree until it eventually fell to the floor. My dad propped the tree up several times. After he had had enough of propping the tree up, he picked up the entire tree, yanked it from the cord I had nailed in the wall, unplugged the lights, opened the front door, and threw the tree, lights, and ornaments onto the yard. What a jackass, I thought.

I had never seen my dad do anything so outrageous. He was drinking gin, but moreover, he was hating buying a house and my mother's shopping. I was let down. I was a child. It was Christmas. I cried, and he told me to go to bed. The next day, icicles and ornaments were scattered across the yard. The neighbors snickered for the next few years that this highly intelligent man was behaving so preposterously. He thought it was funny; he needed to feel like clown. I did not think it funny, and I was charged with cleaning up the disarray in the yard. I considered this the worst Christmas of my childhood and of all times.

Forest Hill, Maryland, was located in the same county as Edgewood. It was northwest of US Route 1 in the southern part of the county. The area was remote, and there was nothing there but the farmland we lived on. The soil was fertile of cow manure. The roads were paved for the impending housing development for Negros. We were no longer living in integrated housing. Homes similar to ours were continuing to be built; there were a total of ten, nothing spectacular. The homes were three-bedroom rangers with modifications of materials used on the interior and exterior of the homes. The lots were three-quarters of an acre to two acres. The development was called Hickory Hills; the area of the county was Hickory, but the post office was Forest Hill. There was a Sinclair gas station and a corner grocery store farther up on US Route 1 on Fountain Green Road. The segregated school I attended was on the same side of US Route 1 as our little development, thus I could walk to school.

Of Time and Spirit

Walking to school seemed surreal after so many years of being bused to maintain segregation in the county. I would have plenty of time on my hands that logically could have been used for studying; however the rural setting generated no inspiration in me. Hickory was nothing but farmland and the smell of cow manure. As we drove down the bumpy country roads, I could smell manure intermixed with intervals of pure fresh country air. I would roll up my windows to keep from being asphyxiated from the manure smells. All that aside, it was the nicest residence of all the places we had ever lived. It was another step up for my mother and my father, for they were now homeowners. I benefitted greatly as well.

My dad would drive my mother and me to see the construction of the house in process every Friday afternoon after they returned from work and ate a quick dinner. It was a pleasant car ride. It was my second trip to the area on those Fridays, in that my school bus transported me to my school across the field from Edgewood. It was a much nicer ride in the car than on the army school bus. My dad wanted to ensure the construction of the house was being done correctly. We did not have premier builders. Our house lacked many of the finishing features of much nicer homes owned by whites. This was hard to achieve when my dad wanted the cheapest of almost everything. All in all, it was a pretty decent house when it was completed—basic and minimal.

As we were driving down the hill, exiting the community after one of my dad's weekly assessments of the house construction, my dad saw one of the other neighbors who had already moved into their new home. He stopped the car to speak to our new neighbor and his wife. My dad introduced himself, my mother, and me. The two couples engaged in friendly conversations for a few minutes. I was seated in the back seat and observed the conversation.

After we bid one another our fair wells and extended congratulations on homeownership, my dad drove away. He spoke of how nice the neighbors were when I blurted out, "They are nice, but that woman is the ugliest woman I have ever seen."

My dad's eyes popped out of his face and his skin turned red-brown. He used all his power to suppress laughter as a result of my comment. My dad was the family humorist and comedian. I had never seen him hold back laughter under any circumstances. He looked as if he was going to explode. He was the leader in our family for making light of every situation, but this time he was straining to hold back his laughter. I was totally not

79

cognitive of my comment and its effect on him. It was an observation, with no harm intended.

My mother immediately lit into me, saying, "Don't you ever let me hear you saying anything like that again, boy! People can't help the way they are born or what they look like. People are born with bowed legs, knocked knees, blindness, cock-eyed, and all kinds of ways. But for the grace of God, it could have been you." She went on and on with me for about ten minutes. I had no realization of what I had said, but when she finished with me, I had a idea.

Then she lit into my father and told him he should be ashamed of himself for laughing. "That's no way to raise a child!" She started in on him and his tongue lashing was equal to mine. When she finished chastising both of us, she was tired and out of breath. She turned her head to the front passenger side window, thinking I would not see her. However, from the back seat, I could see she was struggling to suppress laughter too. She could not help herself, and she quietly burst into laughter too after reflecting on my observation. It was probably the most unkind words she had ever heard me say. She shook her head and said, "You don't ever know what is going to come out of the mouths of these children!"

It was dark by the time we returned home. Everyone had settled down.

The neighbor lady that I commented on became my best friend. She gave her son my first name as his middle name because she thought I was such a nice child. Life is a puzzlement!

There was no question that my dad had outstanding credit to secure a conventional mortgage loan versus a Veterans Administration loan for their house. After six months, the house was finally completed. My mother and my father went to settlement on October 1, 1960. They were forty-one years old. My mother's brother from Washington DC owned a small moving business. He and his men moved us from Edgewood to Hickory. My dad held the greatest admiration for my uncle Bill, a Negro, for having the gumption to start a moving and taxi business in the nation's capital. My dad paid him generously and tipped his movers too.

My dad was accustomed to apartment and city living, but he was in the country now. It was just like his grandparents' farm in Bowie, Maryland. He had enjoyed going to the Enoch Pratt Free Library and learning the labyrinth of any city. From his childhood, he always thought Negros who owned homes were hoity-toity and looked down on him. He never cared to associate with people who thought themselves superior to him. There were family members on his father's side of the family who thought they were better because they were teachers, homeowners, and lighter complexed. Now he was a homeowner, but not by choice. The housing issue was now resolved for him. He was relieved. He didn't notice any difference between paying a mortgage and paying rent. He paid early or definitely on time each month. My mother was happy, and peace was restored at home. The performance of composer Richard Wagner's *Tristan Und Isolde*, "Prelude to Act I," conducted by Leopold Stokowski of the Cleveland Orchestra was restored along with all of my dad's great music. This was a consistent musical theme and served as a background within our new home as well as the old.

The one thing that my dad hated the most about owning the house was cutting the grass. We lived on a three-quarter-acre lot. We had a push lawnmower until our neighbor recommended that my dad purchase a self-propelled power mower. My dad never assigned me the chore of cutting the grass. The neighborhood men were teaching their boys to cut grass. Although I had chores of washing the dishes, taking out the trash, making my bed, my dad did not think cutting the grass was my job.

Our neighbor, and my dad's only best friend, commented to my dad about my not cutting the grass. He thought the boys should learn to cut grass, but my dad passed it off, saying, "Zelma gives the boy the best of everything. He doesn't know how to cut grass." In reality, my dad protected me from anything laborious. He knew I was a mother's boy, and he never interfered with Zelma's child.

I found out through my mother that my dad hated to see the weekends come because he hated to cut the grass. On my own, I attempted to cut the grass one Friday after school while he was at work. When he turned the corner to enter our housing development and saw that the grass had been cut, he was ecstatic. My mother said to me, "I have never seen your father so happy." At last I had pleased my dad. It was one less maintenance task for him. I knew from my parents' disagreements over the house how much my dad hated buying a house. I liked the house and wanted him to keep it. I wanted to take some of the pressure off of him.

In my mind, which my dad never thought I had, I was happy that I had finally done something that pleased him. He said I did a good job and paid me for cutting the grass. The money was in addition to my weekly allowance and became the incentive for me to keep cutting the grass. Every week missing none, the grass was cut, and he paid me. He never stiffed me. The men in the neighborhood thought that he was spoiling me, and their boys were giving them hell for making them cut grass when it was not compulsory for me and got paid too.

I could never hold an intellectual conversation with my dad because I had no interest in scholarship, news, or world events. I was a social child, and for the most part, we had nothing in common. When I had finally performed a function of value to him, and he was happy, I was happy to make a connection with him. I repeated the habit to get his attention. However, he never asked or mandated me to cut the grass. I was thirteen years old, but in his mind, I was Zelma's child.

I was excited that my father and my mother were homeowners, although we were living in the middle of nowhere. We lived about five miles from the town of Bel Air. Some of the schoolboys would hitchhike to Bel Air. I never did. With the exception of visiting the neighbors, there was nothing that stimulated me, not even school.

One of the first social events that we had in the new house was a surprise twentieth wedding anniversary party I hosted. I was thirteen years old. I have no idea how I had the nerve to ask my dad's men friends to provide the liquor and my mother's women friends to cook the food. I provided a contribution from my allowance to the neighbors for their help. I cleaned the house and cut the grass and purchased all the party paper goods.

My dad's men friends knew to bring gin for my dad, his trademark. The party was a success, until one of the men asked my dad if he would do it all over again—get married—and my dad said, "No!"

My mother overheard his response, and that ruined the party for her. Living with my parents could be difficult sometimes. My mother wanted to keep up appearances, and my dad wanted the simplest life he could get. My mother was not the woman who sang: "Give Me the Simple Life." My mother wanted things and to get ahead economically.

The biggest disagreement that my mother and I ever had occurred when she replaced the bedroom furniture where she and my dad slept. One of the shortcomings of our house was that the bedroom closets were small. I had the smallest bedroom but the largest closet, and it was full of clothes for me. My mother took possession of the two smaller closets in each of the other two bedrooms. My dad was relegated to the hall closet that was smaller than the bathroom linen closet. My dad called it his "Ha! Ha! Closet." I did not think it fair, but my mother made the rule, and my dad accepted it. He required so little and accepted so little as far as the house was concerned.

When the oversized five-piece bedroom set was delivered, my mother had planned to give my dad only two drawers of the chest of drawers. I thought this was an opportunity to give my dad more storage spaces. She would still have her triple dresser. My mother did not think that my dad needed more space.

I said nicely, "Mother, give Dad the whole chest of draws."

She replied, "Men don't need that much space. He can use two drawers."

I countered, "Mother, give Dad the whole chest of drawers. You will have the two-bedroom closets, triple dresser, and all he has is the hall closet. He deserves to have the chest of drawers."

She replied to me, "Maurice, your dad does not need that much space!" We went back and forth with the discussion. I couldn't believe that she could not see how unfair she was treating Dad. I knew she was in a constant punishing mode for his perceived infidelities, but how much punishment is enough.

I said firmly, "Mother, Dad gets the whole chest of draws!"

I was really crossing the parent-child line, but she finally said in frustration, "All right, all right, Maurice, he can have the whole set of drawers!"

My dad said nothing through this discourse.

I said to my dad, "Those drawers are yours, Dad!"

Then I broke down and cried, for it took a lot of strength to go up against my mother. My mother was not an ornamental woman. This was our only big disagreement in life. My dad was grateful for the drawers and always said, "He never would have had them if it were not for Maurice."

My dad had never given up his working with the Parent-Teacher Association after my siblings left home. The teachers and the principal of the Central Consolidated School respected my dad's intellect and the urban ideas and sophistication he brought to the rural school.

The teachers and other community leaders requested my dad to take the leadership in composing a letter to J. Millard Tawes, governor of the State of Maryland, requesting a day care center for mentally retarded (nomenclature of that time) children in Northern Maryland.

Governor J. Millard Tawes's executive assistant replied to my dad's request stating the State Department of Mental Hygiene was requesting funds for the establishment of several such day care centers and could be assured that the governor would give every consideration to my dad's request. The letter was signed by Edmund C. Mester, Executives Assistant to the Governor, November 23, 1960. This was great news for a Negro to get a reply from the governor. The governor followed through with several day care centers in the state. One serviced Harford County. My dad was applauded by the community and school leaders.

CHAPTER 7

Two Plates Broken

1960

John Fitzgerald Kennedy, who we called JFK, was the thirty-fifth president of the United States, and our family was happy, and the country seemed to rejoice, although he narrowly defeated Republican opponent Richard Nixon, who was the incumbent vice president. Things were good and looking up for our family. My sister was attending Morgan State College and was reading Kennedy's book *Profiles in Courage*, which was published while JFK was in the Senate. Being our first college graduate in the family, she frequently came home and, while visiting, shared what she learned. She always elevated us with her reading, vocabulary, and exposure to greater intellects. My mother, dad, and I listened with great interest to my sister pontificate about her higher education. My parents and I were galvanized by my sister's learning, for neither of them were college graduates. She even registered for and learned to speak German. She and my dad taught me to play pinochle, a card game she learned in college. My dad was always my partner since I was the newest learner and was not playing to kill, just in case I made a mistake. My sister was one of my key inspirations for attending college. I wanted to be educated like her and have my parents as proud of me as they were of my sister. My brother was stationed in Le Fontainebleau, France, serving in the United States Army.

I was entering junior high school and wanted a typewriter. I usually asked my mother for everything, but she suggested I go to my father for the typewriter. My dad willingly said OK, but I needed to pay for it myself. He thought it was time for me to make my own investments in things that I wanted. I had accumulated a nice little savings account and could afford to purchase a typewriter. He drove me to Baltimore to a pawnshop on Pennsylvania Avenue, the Black commercial district. It was a Baltimore hotspot for Negro nightlife and entertainment and day shopping. For me it was the scariest place I had ever been to in my entire little life. It was unusually hot and stuffy on the streets; the streets were not clean and smelled of alcohol and tobacco. The entrance to the pawnshop had a roll-up security door, and the doormat was dirty and worn. My mother and I had shopped in the nice department stores where there were pristine parking lots, plate glass windows with well-dressed mannequins and figurines. They had escalators. Pennsylvania Avenue was a shock to me.

I had never owned anything used in my life that I knew of. I had no awareness, but I was a snob as a teenager. As we walked into the pawnshop, I looked around with skepticism. All items were behind cases of overly used and scratched plexiglass. When the salesclerk asked what we were looking for, my dad looked at me and said, "Tell the man what you want."

"A portable typewriter," I replied.

The man disappeared and returned to counter with a perfect-looking Smith Corona typewriter in a very smart beige compact carrying case. The salesclerk opened the case and let me type on it. It was in perfect shape. My dad said, "Do you want it?"

I said, "Yes!" I just wanted to escape the pawnshop and Pennsylvania Avenue. Visually, I just did not feel safe and wanted to flee. Knowing full well my dad would protect me, I still want to get out of there.

My dad said, "Well, did you bring your money to pay for it?"

"Yes!" I replied. I paid for the typewriter and learned in the process that it was less than one-half the price of retail at the department stores where my mother and I had shopped around. This was the only thing I ever paid with my money. I used the typewriter day and night. I elected to take a basic and advanced typing course in junior high and high school and received A's consistently. It was the only course in junior high school I showed any interest in and earned A's for. This was the first time in my life I recalled having fun, and it was typing, of all things. This was a skill my dad excelled at the Cortez Peters Business School showing up in his son.

The typewriter went with me to the University of Maryland, where papers were required to be typed. It was a great typewriter, but to date, I have never returned to a pawnshop or Pennsylvania Avenue on purpose. My dad repeated to me throughout my life, "I thought I was a privileged character." I would guess that I was, but not deliberately—it was a by-product of what my mother exposed me to, and I had become accustomed to it.

In June 1961, my dad received from the Department of the Army a certificate in recognition of twenty years of federal service. The recognition did not mean much to him. He was good at his work, but he was not thrilled with what he was doing. Developing chemical weapons that could kill people during a time of war was contrary to his Catholic teaching and the Ten Commandments. He did not see it as making a positive contribution to the world, but most of all, this did not satisfy what he was seeking. He was nonchalant. However, as a Negro family in Harford County, our family was doing very well as a result of his years of labors. Many Negro men were not happy with their jobs, but you had to keep working to live. Partaking in the work of your dreams was not always accessible to Negros even if you had demonstrable qualifications and experience.

There were scores of white families who lived in nicer housing developments, owned nicer homes, drove nicer cars, and were accepted into the county country club. Segregation was still prevalent in Harford County housing, schools, stores, and restaurants. My mother shopped in Baltimore for almost everything except food, because we were still not accepted in most business establishments. I was proud of my dad's adaptability, endurance, and achievement in such an unreceptive environment, especially considering where he started from in his life—a poor Catholic family with many children. My dad had taken us far, and I was one of his prime beneficiaries. I was grateful.

My dad was still having conflicting issues with the teachings of the Catholic Church on the subject of sexuality. He wrote in his journal circa 1960,

> Elizabeth Winship-It is not possible to run out of sperm from masturbating, so there is no need to stop. While some very devout people consider the practice a sin, most professionals dealing with health care believe that it is a normal, natural and healthy way to deal with sexual tensions when other relations are not possible or wise. And despite lingering taboos, 99% of males and most females masturbate at some point in their lives.

In 1962, my dad was trained in supervision by the Army Chemical Center and the Chemical Corps Material Command in Chicago, Illinois. He learned employee relationships, responsibilities, selection, induction, performance appraisal, and safety. He was promoted to supervising engineering assistant. My dad did not like supervision because he was challenged often by white subordinates and nonsubordinates, just as he was in Alabama when he served in the army.

One of my dad's white male subordinates, who thought he should have gotten the position my dad earned, told my dad that he was fired. Right then and there, my dad packed up his desk and locker and started walking off the job. The division chief observed my dad leaving the building and asked him where he was going. My dad said that one of his white subordinates fired him. My dad's superior told him the subordinate had no authority to fire him and to get back to work. My dad knew this but did not like haggling with employees to do their job. He had worked alone and kept to himself and was not in the mood to be the token Negro supervisor. His choice was to walk away. From then forward, it was made known by my dad's superiors to all employees that my dad was the most qualified, hired, and was in charge of his unit. There would be no further dissention in his unit without consequences. "Do I make myself clear?" the division chief stated.

When my dad came home and told my mother what had happened, she said, "Ros? Do you mean to tell me you would have just walked off the job?"

My dad said, "Yes!"

My mother replied, "Well? I can't believe you would have walked off of a good-paying job because of one person's unauthorized remarks, unless you had taken leave from your senses." This was my dad. He would not pick a fight on the job, especially when he wasn't enamored with the work anyway. My dad did a great job, and he knew he did a great job. He was working to simply take care of his wife and children. He was partial to his mental serenity and did not like being detached from it.

During 1963, the army sent my dad to Sciaky Brothers, Inc., Technical Division, to learn Dekatron Machine Theory and Maintenance, and in 1964 to COHU Electronics, Inc., San Diego, California. He had similar discrimination experiences as he had in Foxboro, Massachusetts, and Waterbury, Connecticut. The nearby hotel would not provide accommodations to my dad. The two companies assigned my dad to a

Of Time and Spirit

room within the physical plant of the corporation, not the hotel with the white men. My dad's room was located under the helipad. He was the only Negro. They wanted to ensure he would not succeed in this two-week training by not getting enough rest. He was being trained to weld with lasers. This was considered a highly technical skill, and he needed his rest. In spite of the orchestrated sabotage, my dad succeeded.

These types of injustices were experienced by my dad and many other Negros throughout their lives. Black students, en masse, were leading protests and sit-in demonstrations at lunch counters at North Carolina Agricultural and Technical College, South Carolina State, Southern University, Howard University, Morris-Brown, Spellman, Bennet College, Florida A&M, and other Historically Black Colleges and Universities during the 1964 civil rights movement. If you were black and not picketing, something was considered wrong with you. Black students felt the purpose of higher education was to do something concrete; equality was the reason for the protest. The young black students considered themselves the engine for this change. Violence and resistance were enforced by white legislators, local police, state troopers, and the National Guard. Lockdowns were imposed. In 1963, President John F. Kennedy was assassinated. My world felt dark for a long time afterward. My brother was back from France, and I was the first to inform him of the Kennedy assassination. He was sitting in a bathtub of water, and I made the announcement through the partially opened door.

During my primary and secondary school years, my school sponsored day-long bus excursions to Washington DC, Hershey Park, Pennsylvania, and other nearby amusement parks and recreational sites. My dad consistently packed the family's one insulated plastic Coca-Cola lunch bag with sandwiches and chips for me to eat during the day. He always gave me more than enough spending money for the entry fees and amusement rides. He sent me off on my day-long adventures in good spirits. He was happy that I was growing up and finally showing signs of not needing to be around my mother for everything. I am positive my mother was happy too. Never with words had my dad showed signs of being proud of me that I could feel. He was encouraging me to grow up and move on.

When I was fifteen, my mother thought I had been a mother's boy long enough. She told my dad in my presence, "It is time for you to take over and teach the boy about becoming a man."

At this point in my life, I had spent very little face-to-face time with my dad. I hardly knew him. I wasn't sure that I liked some of the positions he took in the family. I wasn't sure I even liked him. For years, I was ridiculed by him, and at times, he could be cold and indifferent toward me, or so I thought. Up to this point, I had accompanied my mother to her hairdresser, food shopping, and we had traveled together to every shopping mall in the region. She purchased all my clothes, packed my lunch for school, taught me to pray every night, and made sure I was bathed and had taken cod-liver oil and scotch emulsion to ward off colds and sickness. She smeared a light coating of Vaseline on my face on the cold winter mornings when it was much too cold to be standing outside at the bus stop. "You are spoiled," she would say. So now this man was going to take over? How was that going to happen? This was an odd feeling for me in that I did not know what to expect. I had been with my mother my whole life. I never had a babysitter, ever.

My dad could feel my resistance to his teaching me anything, and he had little patience with me, but he tried. He would gently tell me I was stupid rather frequently. Historically, my brother and my sister imitated him. They were never too enamored with me, nor me with them.

When the time was drawing near for me to get a driver's license, he taught me to read the motor oil stick to make sure there was always enough oil in the car. He said if I ever got a flat tire, don't call him, thus he taught me to change a tire. Checking the oil and changing tires were of little interest to me; but being able to get out of Hickory was essential, so I carefully learned automobile maintenance. My dad taught me to drive and to perfectly parallel-park. He also taught me to shave and to tie a Windsor Knot.

I had wandering eyes while driving. My dad ordered me to keep my eyes on the road. My dad was an overly careful driver. Never in his eighty-one years do I recall him being involved in an accident or being issued a speeding violation. He always followed the speed limit and was viewed in my family as the driver who never had an accident but caused many. He was slow and methodical. I think his vision was an issue too that was never discussed.

When I was sixteen, my dad insured me on his two cars and got me my learner's permit. On the day of the driver's exam, I passed the parking test but failed the written test. I was teenaged-style distraught. I was really anxious and in a big hurry to get my license.

I was keenly looking forward to retaking the written test the following week. The driver's test was offered once per week, and a week for me was too long to wait. My dad was not available to take me to get my driver's test the following week. He said that I could wait two weeks to take the written test. He saw no harm in my waiting an additional week. He thought it reasonable. I did not and felt outdone that he did not make my driving test a priority. I wanted my license as soon as possible. Most teens feel the same.

After my mother and my dad departed home for work that morning, I was trying to figure out how I could get to the National Guard Armory in Bel Air to retake the written test. After a little thinking, I walked across the street and asked our neighbor Mr. Clark, who was the driver education instructor at Havre de Grace Consolidated School, the other nearby segregated school, to take me in his car to retake my written test. He said OK, and I took the written test and passed, and my driver's license was issued to me.

When my mother and my dad arrived home from work that afternoon, I proudly announced that I had passed the written examination and was issued my driver's license. My dad was furious that I had maneuvered a way to get my license. His thinking was, if he was not available, I was to wait until he was available. I was not to independently go out on my own as a minor and get a license. He was not pleased with me or the neighbor. He had a fuming chat with the neighbor. In my dad's eyes, I was disobedient, and possibly, it was an experience he wanted to have with me.

My mother, on the other hand, was as proud as could be. She thought that I was a timid child with no spine or backbone. She said to me privately, "I am proud of you. Never let someone tell you what you can't do. Always figure out a way to get what you want done on your own. Learn to stand on your own two feet."

She had a chat with my dad to calm him down. "The boy is growing up! He is showing some signs of independence. Leave him alone."

"I keep telling you that you don't know anything about raising children. Children are thinking and scheming while you are asleep! They are always trying to outslick you!"

She was grateful to have an avenue to detach me from her apron strings. I was grateful to be liberated from Hickory Hills. My dad was like the King of Siam: obey the rules!

As a student of a Catholic school and a soldier in the army, my dad was accustomed to authority, order, and control. He expected absolute obedience from me. After this driver's license encounter, if maturity or forgiveness was necessary from my dad, he demonstrated both, or maybe what my mother said to him packed some weight. Regardless, I had my license. Another family crisis that blew over.

My dad eventually let me drive him everywhere. It was also a chance for him to sit in the back seat of the car and sip gin from his flask as I drove. Once he thought I had enough experience, he allowed me to take the car independently, with restrictions to start and a "must" requirement that the car have the same amount of gasoline in the tank when I returned it as it had when I drove it away from the house. He would be pretty salty if this requirement was not met. It was rare that I ever forgot this detail. I had to pay for my gas with my allowance. This ensured I was not going too far because I wouldn't have the necessary money to stray too far.

Another one of his joys of my learning to drive occurred when my school was closed during the summer months. My dad would let me drive him to work in the morning and come back to pick him up in the afternoon. His only "must" requirement here was not to be late picking him up. My dad was a stickler for time, relentless. He was like this by his personal habits and was wedded to preciseness of time and order by training. I got plenty of his Saturday errands completed for him during weekdays, giving him more downtime during the weekends to enjoy his reading, writing, and classical music. He appreciated my taking on his odd tasks.

As a general rule, I did not feel comfortable talking to my dad. Before I could complete a thought, he had made a judgment and gave me his answer. My style of communication was often ambiguous and long winded, and my dad did not have time to listen to the whole story. Thus, he never knew of my inner feelings.

Nationally, public schools were ruled integrated in 1954 after the *Brown v. the Board of Education* Supreme Court ruling. Harford County was slow to integrate schools. Many white people were not ready for integration, and in some instances, black parents were reluctant to integrate for fear of repercussions to their children, as was the case with my mother. She did not want me to attend white schools unchaperoned. My brother, sister, and I all attended the Central Consolidated School for Negros in the southern location of the county, and she felt that was some buffer for me, although I was in elementary school while they were in high school. The school housed grades one through twelve in one physical plant. She was no longer a stay-at-home mother so she wanted me to continue in the segregated schools where she knew and familiar with the teachers and the principal.

After my parents moved from Edgewood to Forest Hill, they were approached by white school board members and asked if I would be one of the Negro children to help integrate the county schools. I was being handpicked because of my dad's reputation as a respectable Negro in the county. My dad absolutely did not want me to attend. He was bitter and frustrated with the slow implementation and enforcement of federal laws in Harford County. He also did not think I could survive the horrors of integration and racism as he had experienced in the military and in the civilian workplace. I had been sheltered by both parents and was a mother's boy; however, my parents checked in with me, and they asked me if I wanted to attend the white school, and I said, "Yes!"

Even as a child, I knew there were huge distinctions between Negro life and the white world. A few episodes of *Leave It to Beaver*, *I Love Lucy*, and *The Mickey Mouse Club* let me know that I was not living the life of a white person in America. I wanted more for myself, and I wanted to go mainstream. A segregated life held nothing for me in my situation and where I lived.

It was 1964, and I was the only Negro student in my eleventh-grade class of 460 students at the Bel Air High School. It was somewhat late in my schooling to be making such a drastic transition; I knew none of the teacher or students. This was a huge risk I volunteered to undertake. It would have been easier academically if I had mainstreamed in first grade in 1954 without mayhem. My mother offered me the option of attending the John Carroll School, which was new at the time, opening in 1960. It was a private Catholic school for grades 9–12 located closer to our house than Bel Air High School; but I thought with my dad's apprehensions and my average grades, I'd better leave well enough alone.

John Carroll was linked to the Archdiocese of Baltimore. Blacks continued to sit in the back of both Catholic churches we attended—Saint Ignatius and Saint Margaret's. Whites were no less prejudiced because they were Catholics or churchgoers. With the public school, I would have the federal government to back me up; with the Catholic school, I would have only the pope, and he was unreachable.

As with my driver's license, my mother supported my decision to attend Bel Air High School. She told my dad, "Let the boy learn to make his own decisions."

My dad was really hesitant about my going and stayed mindful of what I was doing and what I was learning. Periodically, he would ask, "What are they teaching you down there at that school, boy?" I don't care how old I got—everything my parents said to me was punctuated with the word *boy*! For the most part, I was as happy as a lark and lived up to my average grades, no better and no worse. There was moderate resistance to my attending Bel Air High School, but mostly from the school principal; however, liberal teachers stood guard on me and watched how I was treated. My twelfth-grade homeroom teacher and history teacher had a confederate name: Robert E. Lee Ross. I loved Mr. Ross, and Mr. Ross loved me.

When the white students at Bel Air High were going to Rehoboth Beach, Ocean City, and Virginia Beach for summer recess, I wanted to go too. The beaches at that time were segregated. Blacks were not allowed or welcomed at those beaches. Negros were relegated to Sandy Point or Carr's Beach. They were substandard by comparison. My parents never patronized these beaches. My dad would, however, filled the car with gas, pack a big lunch, and give me money to go to the white beaches on my own but instructed me not to get into swim trunks or get into the water. Although I never enjoyed the ocean waters, I had the pleasure of saying when I returned to school that I too had been to the same beaches as my classmates. I walked the boardwalk and would purchase a hot dog or cotton candy. I would stay a few hours and return home. In my teenage thinking, it made me feel less discriminated against. My dad would have called such thinking, "Stupid!"

Although my dad taught me how to drive and maintain a car, it did amaze me that he trusted me to drive one of his cars across the Chesapeake Bay Bridge alone. I did not recall my siblings having this amount of freedom unless they did it unauthorized. Times were slowly changing, but moreover, I was a free spirit and tried to be brave.

During this same time, 1964, my dad was sent to COHU Electronics, Inc., San Diego, California, to study the theory of operation, calibration, and maintenance of television systems. When he returned home, he seemed somewhat invigorated. He fell in love with a flower he had never seen before in the East Coast, called the bird of paradise. He thought it was the most magnificent flower he had ever seen. He brought a cutting of the flower home for my mother and me to see. Every time I see one of these flowers, I think of my dad and his reaction and appreciation of this flower. My mother cared little about flowers. She liked money.

My dad, although very secure financially, would accept odd jobs around Harford County for old white people when they asked him. He interestingly did yard work for others with pay and hated working in his yard. He catered parties in red, white, or black uniforms to earn extra money. He asked if I wanted to go along. I said yes to his offers because he was my father and he was reaching out to me. He wanted to teach me how to hustle a few dollars. I had no work experience outside of the home. I had higher ambitions and never wanted to cater parties for a living, but that was my dad's point—he wanted to emphasize how unhappy I would be in a low-paying job, factoring in his assessment of my ambition and the exposure my mother had provided. He knew I liked expensive things. I recognized he had good points; we had nothing in common at this point, but he was a perfect provider for our family, and he taught me a lot. Sometimes I learned things to survive that I did not want to learn. I never knew before accepting these odd job offers that he was going to pay me for my work. I thought the request was more or less a gentle directive. He paid me generously every single time, usually half and half, plus tips. He would tell my mother that I was a good worker. I was astonished that he complimented me. I usually felt he saw me as a lightweight and not intellectually substantial.

I was a money-hungry teenager. I was offered a part-time job after school at the Bel Air Bowling Alley. The job necessitated my driving one of my dad's cars to get to the job. My grades were only fair, and my dad thought that I should use the time to study for better grades; but I begged, and he relented with the stipulation that if my grades fell, the job was out. I think he wanted me to graduate high school. Some days I didn't think my dad cared. At this juncture, both of my parents allowed room for me to fail if I made dumb choices. It was better I fail while I was at home than after I left home and needed to return. Neither parent wanted their children to return home permanently after reaching adulthood, nor did we.

As a teenager, I could get pretty moody, sometimes for up to five days. I had read that being a teenager was the most difficult time in the child's development process. If the information was correct, it applied to me. It annoyed my mother no end that I would show any signs of discontent, considering she bent over backward to give me everything. Nevertheless, when the end of the week rolled around, my dad would give me my weekly allowance and extra money for cutting the grass. It shamed me to accept my allowance. When my mood subsided, I asked my dad, "Why did you give me my allowance when I had been in such a miserable mood all week?"

He replied, "You did the work."

What was implied was that I had completed all my chores and cut the grass. He did not require me to be happy while I performed these tasks. Most children would have been punished or chastised for pouting for a week. My mother did not think I deserved anything. I felt bad about being moody. But my dad was reasonable. His being reasonable was my punishment.

Anticipating graduation from Bel Air High School for eleventh and twelfth grades, I wanted to apply to the University of Maryland–College Park, a historically white university that had a larger student population than Edgewood or Forest Hill. My mother by this time had accumulated her own money. She expressed to me that I could attend college anywhere I wanted to go. My dad thought my attending the University of Maryland was outrageous. He did not like the idea at all and created a stink. After a very heated family debate between my mother, my father, and my sister, my sister, the honor student and college graduate who my dad had respect for, came to my defense, just as my mother had with my driver's license and my volunteering to integrate the eleventh grade at Bel Air High School. My sister said to my dad, "Let Maurice go! He can do it!" My sister settled the discussion, and I applied and was accepted to the University of Maryland–College Park as my first choice of undergraduate institutions. I had applied at Lincoln University, where another classmate was accepted and graduated.

My dad had no respect for my opinion or my mother's opinion on this subject since he did not consider us as bright. Moreover, he did not see me as academically competitive to succeed in one of the top ten largest public universities in the country and the white environment. I was a C student every year from first grade to twelfth grade, whether segregated or integrated. It took my sister to convince him to agree to my attending, although my mother paid every cent of my tuition, room, and board. My mother and my dad had decided and arranged earlier in their marriage that my mother would pay for my brother to attend college, my dad would pay for my sister, and she would pick up the tab on me. He didn't agree to my going to the University of Maryland, but at least he did not have to pay. I think he was unhappy with me being there for the entire four and one-half years I was an undergraduate student. My dad was a much better student than me, and I think my attending the University of Maryland opened the wound of his lost opportunity at Saint Emma's Military Academy and his being rejected from Officer's Candidate School in the United States Army. It was hard for him to see an average kid (even his kid) get the opportunities that he was denied.

By 1966, one academic year later, I was not doing well academically at the university. Attending the university was my first experience living away from home. I was a social being, and I thought I could charm my way through school. I learned that I was not at home, and nobody cared about my charm. I was not that charming. I came home almost every weekend on the Greyhound bus. My dad would pick me up from the bus stop at the corner of Richardson's Pharmacy, Main Street, and take me home. We said little to each other; I felt we forced a few words here and there. I was in school, but to him, I was not learning anything. I had no good grades to share. It was an unspoken, *I told you so* moment.

During this time too, tension was added to my being a student at the University of Maryland due to the Vietnam War. The war started November 1, 1955, and ended in April 30, 1975. The war was taking place during my college years. My mother absolutely, positively did not want me to go into the military because she felt I would never make it; and if I did, I would come back shell-shocked like my dad's brother. My dad, on the other hand, was ready for me to grow up and be a man. When my grades slipped and I was on academic probation, he literally took me to the army induction station in Bel Air to board a bus to Fort Holabird for my annual physical examination for induction into the army. Camp Holabird was renamed Fort Holabird in 1950. The United States Army Intelligence School and Counter-intelligence Records Facility was based at this location until it was transferred to Fort Huachuca, Arizona, in 1972. It was, conversely, used as an Armed Forces Examining and Entrance Station (induction station). My dad seemed to resent me being spoiled any longer, and I was getting too old, although he contributed to it. Going into the army was what he was forcing me to do, and the truncation of my college education mattered little to him because he could not see where I was making the best use of it anyway.

I, on the other hand, did not care about going into the army. I preferred finishing undergraduate school first; that seemed more sequential. I would have chosen the air force after finishing college, not the army. I had all kinds of conflicted feelings wanting both parents happy. Ultimately, the army deferred me due to hypertension. This decision made by the United

States Army made it easy for me to strive toward my mother's dream of all three of her children graduating college.

She believed, as her father had taught her, that if you give your children a chance to make it in the world, when they leave home, they have enough undergirding and knowledge that, hopefully, they would make good decisions. My mother also wanted to be assured that none of her children returned home with wife and/or children at some later point in her life. She wanted to totally complete her job and be finished with children. They would have enough education to make it on their own and not blame her for not preparing them for the world.

Both parents had the same end result: "Break a plate!" My dad's objective was moving the children to the outward position sooner, and my mother's objective was to move the children to the outward position after being adequately prepared. My dad once again felt defeated, but I had nothing to do with the army's decision. This period was really disruptive to my undergraduate studies as there was conflicting thinking from my parents, as there was about my driver's license, building the house, and other family matters.

I always felt sorry for my dad, but I never knew how to comfort him because he was not comfortable within himself. I always made a special effort every year to leave campus and come home for my dad's birthday in April, even if his birthday fell on a weekday. He thought that was stupid too. He thought that time should be used for studying. I would stop at Hutzler's downtown to buy him a gift. I worked for Hutzler's Men's Department for two summers and at Christmas break. I was at home for every holiday and semester break for four and one-half years. My mother, my dad, and my sister all had input into deciding what to do with Maurice and his education.

My dad had been promoted to supervisor and was sent to training in effective governmental writing. He learned writing for shortness, simplicity, strength, and sincerity. The Department of the Army presented my dad with a certificate of completion in the Effective Writing Course. The certificate was issued by the United States Army, Edgewood Arsenal, Maryland; Baxter L. Poling, chief, Training and Development; and William J. Morrisroe, lieutenant colonel, MPC Chief of Staff on March 17, 1967. My dad never shared his happiness or glee about being selected for these opportunities. He was not boastful; he just did his job, exceptionally.

To my knowledge, my dad only had one best friend, Thomas Nottage. He was called Tommy, and as a child, I called him Mr. Tommy. He was a tall and heavy man; he had smooth, shiny, dark skin; full lips; and impeccably white teeth. His teeth grew slanted to one side. He was a big man. He had the habit of taking his right hand and rubbing his large stomach. He was just as robust in his rear. He was a happy man and always had a generous, receptive smile. Tommy was from Nassau and graduated from North Carolina A&T University.

Mr. Tommy was college educated, but my mother thought he was not as bright as he claimed to be to be college educated. He was a braggart too, my mother thought. She challenged him one day on his boastfulness. She dared that she could beat him in a race down to the foot of the hill of our backyard. Our house was situated on a three-quarter-acre lot. It was a stretch. I could not believe my mother had the boldness to make such a challenge to a man or woman. He and my mother ran. They were neck and neck during the race. He won by inches. My mother did not do poorly, for she was ten to fifteen years older than Mr. Tommy. It was a sight to behold. My dad laughed his head off. I thought it was ludicrous.

My mother thought that my dad never associated with people on his intellectual level. She saw Mr. Tommy as kind and generous, but a lightweight compared to her husband. My dad still liked substantial conversations, classical music, literature, and art, of which Mr. Tommy showed no knowledge of and little interest; but nevertheless, my dad liked Mr. Tommy. He accepted Mr. Tommy as is, and vice versa. There was never a problem or an unkind word between them.

They would commiserate while doing yard work on the weekends; they drank liquor and talked about women. Tommy brought a riding lawnmower and called my dad cheap when my dad refused to buy one when my dad could more likely afford a riding lawnmower when Mr. Tommy couldn't afford the one he owned. With me away in college, my dad had to resume cutting the grass.

When the Plymouth Valiant made its debut, Mr. Tommy liked the reviews of the car and was beginning to feel the financial pinch of homeownership, needing an economy car, compared to his 8-cylinder Ford. Mr. Tommy and his wife were younger and liked to live large. Up to this time, my dad only purchased used Chevrolets. Mr. Tommy wanted my dad to get up off of some of his money in that my dad earned more money. He thought my dad was tight and should be less conservative. He challenged my dad to buy a new car. He said, "I will buy a 'new' Valiant if you buy one."

My dad sprung! They got matching cars in different colors. Never had I seen my dad do anything like that before. He had discretionary money at this point. My dad negotiated the deal with the dealer since the two men were buying two new cars on the same day. They each got a lower price. The difference was that my dad paid cash, but this was his first new car, ever. The Valant was a compact car—cheap but served the purpose. I drove it fast and hard. I liked the push-button gears on the dash. It was fun, but not sporty like the Mustang.

Mr. Tommy had a sister in New York City that he wanted to visit, but moreover, to get away from his wife and children. He wanted my dad to ride along for company. Mr. Tommy suggested that while on their visit, they could also see a New York Giants game. Mr. Tommy was a big spender and said he would buy my dad's entrance ticket. He knew my dad was not into contact sports. Mr. Tommy had a great interest in seeing the Giants play, but not my dad, for he was not a football fan. He liked swimming and golf. My dad made the trek to New York with Mr. Tommy anyway, just for the fun of it and to get out of the house. My dad was never the type to spend that kind of money on recreation. He was doing well at work, settled in the house, and receiving training after training, receiving promotion after promotion, so he splurged on this trip to the Big Apple with his friend. My dad, however, was the type to take his own money to return home, just in case anything happened along the journey. My dad had been exposed to enough people who travelled on a shoestring, and he never wanted to get caught stranded anywhere.

After spending the day with his sister, Mr. Tommy and my dad attended the Giants game. They were seated in the bleachers and during all of the excitement, coupled with the long drive, consumption of liquor, and talk of women, Mr. Tommy said to my dad halfway through the game, near intermission, that he had a headache. He suddenly slumped his head in my dad's lap and died in my dad's arms. He had a massive stroke. Mr. Tommy was very down to earth, honest, and was a good neighbor and friend to my dad. Mr. Tommy had integrity. They could relate. Like the death of his sister Rosalie, who died my dad processed Mr. Tommy's death in acute thought, stillness, and silence. He had lost his only true friend. It was really a sad day, and it remained sad for many days after. This was a blow, and it left my dad in wonderment and puzzlement.

Of Time and Spirit

During the summer of my sophomore year at the University of Maryland, I got a summer job at Interpace Construction as a steel welder. I wanted to buy a car to have on campus. Interpace paid great money. I figured I could save enough to get a car to take back to college in the fall. I asked my dad if I could accept the job for the summer, and he agreed. A hard hat was provided by the job, but I needed steel-toed boots to start. My dad purchased the new steel-toed boots for me. My dad, for some reason unknown to me, purchased good shoes for his children. He thought feet were important, and my dad had neat feet. The factory was hot, and I had never seen men as dirty as these men. They wore the same overalls day after day. The work of making steel-lined concrete tubing for underground water and sewers drains was hard and dirty. It was an assembly-line work. When the night shift ended, I was filthy dirty, and it was not the kind of work that you could take a shower to remove the dirty off of your body. I worked the 8:00 p.m. to 4:00 a.m. shift. At 5:00 a.m., I needed to sit in a tub of hot water and scrub; and it didn't care how much soap I used or what type of soap—the tub had a black ring in it every night/morning. By the time I was clean and had brushed my nail and clipped them, got some sleep, and arose to eat, it was time to go back to work again. It was the best sleep I ever had in my life because I had never been as tired as when I worked at Interpace. I felt like a block of concrete when I slept after work. I can't image that I did not snore; it was a deep sleep.

When I asked my dad if I could quit the job, he said yes. He added that he didn't think I would last that long. He said this was the kind of work I was going to need to do if I didn't pull your grades up in school. He was happy that I had a taste for hard work. I lasted only two weeks on the job and never saved enough money to buy a car to take back to school in the fall. I applied for a job at Hutzler's in Towson, Maryland. I worked in the men's department. I was clean and well-dressed each day and worked in a clean environment. I loved the work, but it paid minimum wage.

Before work one afternoon at Interpace, I visited one of my mother and father's friends whom I liked. Although she was my parents' age, I always saw her as a friend. She liked me, and I liked her. I babysat her daughter as a teenager and washed her '98 Oldsmobile. She always paid me fairly. She talked to me like all the time, as if I were an adult. I think she liked children, but if not, she liked me.

She had been a very kind adult figure to me throughout my childhood. I called her Miss Dot. In our brief conversation before I departed her home to go to work at my steel welder's job, she shared with me that my dad said to her, "Maurice will never make it at the University of Maryland." If I had been in poor health, I would have had a heart attack and died.

I was stunned and really had to contain myself from the sting of her words. Her words hit me harder than anything in my life. Had my dad made it public that he did not believe in me? My body grew warm with rage. I was aware that my dad had little faith in my academic abilities, but never did I think he would put his thoughts into words and announce them to the public. I knew I was not a great student. I was OK with being a good student. I liked myself. I knew I had a friendly personality and great social skills. Average students are often more well-rounded and less intense than subject-matter specialty students. I like being well-rounded. My dad did not understand me or value any worth I may have had, for he was driven by excellence.

I could not drive myself to the job or get to a telephone booth fast enough that afternoon to call my mother and tell her what I had just heard. I was deeply hurt, more hurt than by anything my dad had ever said to me. In retrospect, it was kind of ridiculous on my part. I was twenty years old, wearing a size 13 shoe, and a big afro, crying my eyes out to my mother. How pitiful was that? Regardless, in that moment, I resented my dad for what he had said about me outside of the family.

My mother consoled me by saying, "Maurice, don't pay your father any attention. He doesn't know what he is talking about. He doesn't know anything about raising children. It's just that gin he drinks that's talking!" My mother's intentions were good, but her words did not soothe my wounded feelings. I chose to believe the family friend and neighbor because I knew my dad could be cold-bloodedly honest with his belief about anyone, and I was no exception. He honestly thought I would never make it to graduation from the University of Maryland–College Park. In addition, my mother wasn't in the mood to referee another dissention between my father and me.

Considering my dad did not approve of my attending the university in the first place, and considering he was a man of good judgment, I thought that perhaps he could be right. That infuriated me more. In my stubbornness and determination, I knew for sure that I did not want him to be right. He was never pleased with my academics. I wasn't an academic like him or my sister, nor did I want to be like either of them. I thought them book smart but never having the social skills I possessed. There was a place for me somewhere in the world.

Of Time and Spirit

From the beginning of my freshman year, I was on-and-off academic probation. The adjustment for me coming from principally segregated schools was extremely difficult. I was an average student in an average segregated public school. I did not attend Catholic school as my dad had. The University of Maryland was above average, and the bar was higher. I needed to catch up to the new bar of average. I thought socialization was a part of the education process, and as useful as book learning. I was socializing more than studying. My dad thought I was wasting time and money.

In the middle of my struggles at the university, my grade point average dropped below 2.0 for a second time. The selective service directed me to report to Fort Holabird for a second annual physical examination for induction into the army. I was being drafted. This was still during the Vietnam War years.

My mother cried and told my father he had to do something. "That boy is not prepared to go into the army!"

My dad replied, "Zelma, the boy has got to go."

"But that boy can't make it in no army!" she cried.

For me it was like a scene from *Gone with the Wind* when the white slave master separated the colored child from its mother. My dad had no problem with my going into the army. He was frustrated and firm. He was sick of me wasting money. He wanted to break my plate too.

My dad did not think I could make it at the University of Maryland; my mother did not think I would make it in the army. They both saw me as disabled—one mentally and one physically. I was the child my mother said she never wanted to have; and from my dad's OCS timeline, he got out of the army on a dependency clause at the time my mother was pregnant with me. Interestingly, I thought I would have done well in both the academic and military settings because I knew how to get along with people. The only problem now was I wanted to finish college, but I was not paying one copper cent.

My spirits were low, and my dreams of graduating college were looking dim. My dad and I were silent as he drove me to the bus station for my induction again. My mother was at home crying.

I was bused to Fort Holabird for the day. I took the annual physical examination and failed due to the surgery I had for a plantar wart from the university swimming pool. I was informed that I would not be called back for further reexamination. I returned to the university.

CHAPTER 8

Breaking Plate Number 3-Mine!

1968

In June 1968, my dad made the county news.

> *Aegis*, Bel Air, Maryland, "Makes Roll" – James R.
> Dorsey, Sr., a member of the Weapons Development
> and Engineering Laboratories at Edgewood Arsenal,
> had his name added to the roll of economy champions
> in the Pentagon for a suggestion credited with saving the
> government close to $14,000. His idea called for having
> cryogenic refrigerators installed as leak detector cold traps,
> which would provide more efficient results than the liquid
> nitrogen system formerly used.

The Department of the Army officially commended my dad for
submitting his suggestion, which was adopted. He was issued a Certificate
of Achievement: "Better Product and Service Reduction Cost," Frank
G. White, Major General, USA, Commanding General, United States
Army Munitions Command, November 20, 1968. I must say that I had
no idea how to be happy for my dad because I did not know what he had
accomplished. Engineering was well out of my range of thinking or inquiry
and contributed to my lack of understanding of him.

Of Time and Spirit

On the weekends when I returned home from college, my black and white friends would visit with me at my parents' home. I was happy to invite them because I was proud of my parents' home. My mother had appointed the house beautifully. My mother put on a spread for each of the guys that visited. She also did my laundry while I was there. She was extremely giving and hospitable to my friends. My mother enjoyed the company of the young college guys. She talked and asked questions of each of them for hours at a time just as she and I had done over my lifetime. There were always clean sheets for their beds, and she prepared enough food for hungry college guys. My mother was happy that I was developing friendships. I had none in my childhood.

My dad was not rude to my college mates, but he was not as thrilled as my mother that I brought friends home. He asked me when my friends were ever going to invite me to their homes. My dad was sarcastic at times and reminded me of Archie Bunker. He made a good point. A few of the guys had invited me to their homes, but in that my dad and I seldom communicated, he did not know. Some did not invite me to their home, and they were the ones he was referring to. Some of my college friends had cars on campus and were doing me a favor of driving me home. After his question permeated my brain, I stopped inviting the guys home. He somehow took the joy out of things I enjoyed. I suspect he wanted me to be happy, but at my expense, not his. He did not have the luxury life I was living in college. I am sure it was hard for him to see me get so much when he got so little and deserved so much more. My dad saw me as living a charmed life, and it was. That was what college life was for some students. This was the last chance in life with limited to no major responsibility. I wanted to enjoy university student life. I was in college. In his mind, college was for learning only. We could never seem to come together and stay together. I wanted him to be happy and encouraging for me. His sense of no-nonsense was firm and intact. I was too social and playful for my dad. He wanted me to be more serious.

By the time I had hit my junior year in college, 1968, I was beginning to get adjusted to the rigorous academic and social life at Maryland. I was never too popular, but I was likable, and I could get a date to go to the movies or a campus function. I spent most of my time with my male friends. It was sort of a balancing act with my black friends, my white friends, my Jewish friends, my buddies, my girlfriends, my straight friends, and my gay friends. It was a balancing act because I had never put in words that I was gay. Gay was my stronger proclivity. I wanted to get along in all groups, thus I floated between them.

Athletic events were a big thing on Maryland's campus. I was never much of an athlete and attended few to none of the athletic events on campus. The NCAA Basketball Tournament was being held at North Carolina A&T State University, a historically black college in Greensboro, North Carolina. The University of Maryland was playing in the tournament. All of the black students were urging me to attend to support the precious few black players, but in my heart, it was not a place I would have felt comfortable for any sustained period of time. In most instances, I didn't know the basics of sporting games. But I felt obligated to go to support the university team spirit and to support the black players as well.

My mother and father sent me spending money every two weeks. Their checks were just as punctual as a government check. However, my spending money was not enough for a trip to North Carolina. I knew my parents were working hard and making a sacrifice to send me to college, thus I knew not to ask for anything extra. I was getting over big time as it was. I still felt compelled to at least show my face and be a part of the tournament.

So, I asked my mother if I could go, and she immediately redirected me to my father for the money. She said, "Oh, baby doll! Mother doesn't have that kind of money. You will need to ask your father for something like that."

My mother financed 90 percent of my wants; my dad financed 100 percent of all my needs. I was not accustomed to asking my dad for anything at all throughout my life except that gingerbread cookie. My dad was very conscious in the management of money, thus I knew not to ask him for anything; but this one time, I timidly tiptoed; held my head down with no eye contact, rather pitiful, my voice cracking; and I finally approached my dad as he was concentrating on an article he was reading in the newspaper and listening to classical music. I said, "Dad, can I go to the NCAA Basketball Tournament in Greensboro, North Carolina?" Anticipating a firm, deliberate "No" response, I steeled myself.

He looked up at me and said very calmly, "How much does it cost?"

I replied, "I don't know."

He then replied, "Well, you figure out how much it will cost. Then I will let you know if you can go."

Of Time and Spirit

I loved and had the best of everything as a middle-class child. I proceeded to get the cost of an Eastern Airline Whisper Jet ticket and the cost of a Ford Torino rental car. My mother had never been on an airplane, and neither one of them ever rented a car.

With pure panic, I approached my dad for a second time to submit the cost of my travel. I anticipated rejection when he said, "Where are you sleeping?"

I said, "We are bunking in the dormitory with the other guys. There is no cost."

My dad pulled out his checkbook and wrote me a check with a substantial amount of extra money, stating, "You did not include money for food." He said, "Here, cash this check and you can go!" Instantaneously, I jumped for joy and said thank you, but before I could get upstairs to my bedroom, I was uncontrollably crying. I never expected him to say yes.

For some reason, I felt unacceptable to my dad. Through all my years of living with him and as kind as he could be to me, he could be equally crushing too. If he had said no, then I would have told my friends at Maryland that I couldn't afford to attend the event. It would have been legitimate explanation; at least I attempted to procure funds. That would have been an acceptable reason because surely, many other black students couldn't afford to attend either.

Years later, I asked my dad why he approved such an expensive trip when I could have taken a Greyhound Bus or hustled a ride, and he replied, "Because, Maurice, you never ask for anything." I never knew that I could ask for anything. He had indoctrinated his children to think he wanted to "break a plate" when we were eighteen, and he wanted us out of his house. How was I to know I could approach him?

He would also tell us, "You have Christmas and birthday every day that the rent is paid and there is food on the table!" My takeaway from his comments was to not ask for anything. I had never asked for anything such as this before. I thought his response to my request was over-the-top.

I flew via Eastern Airlines to North Carolina. I rented a car nicer than any car my dad ever owned. I attended the game. I was visually recorded by my college mates as having taken part in the university spirit and supporting the black players from Maryland.

The real irony of the hoopla and fanfare surrounding my need to participate in this student event occurred when the game was over. After the game, the celebrations began. All I did was watch the guys and girls

107

who were either drinking alcohol, smoking pot, dancing close, and/or getting laid. I sat alone. I had no girlfriend or boyfriend, I didn't smoke pot. I felt isolated; it was a lonely experience for me after all the extremes I went through to attend. I should have followed my gut feelings and stayed on campus. The experience for me was a waste of time and money, but you could not have convinced me of that before I departed for the travel. I don't recall who was playing or who won the game.

In December 1969, my dad was an expert now in the field of electronics, laser, calibration, and industrial instruments. He was invited to Honeywell, Inc., in Fort Washington, Pennsylvania, to learn Electronik 15, 18 Industrial Instrumentation. Like all of his previous trainings sponsored by the government, he satisfactorily completed his course of study. He was closing in on his thirty years of civilian service for the Army Weapons Development and Engineering Laboratories. He was proud of what he had accomplished, but this work never truly fulfilled him, and he still, after all of this time, was in wonderment and search of what his inner spirit wanted. He was in a class of nineteen men. In the group photograph, my dad was the only Negro, the most well-groomed and best dressed. He had on a dark suit and hand-starched white shirt that my mother ironed, dark socks, and polished shoes. My dad called socks stockings. He had a fresh haircut and neatly trimmed mustache and wore black horn rimmed eyeglasses. My dad remained a very handsome man as he aged. He was considered an acceptable colored, although he did not fall heir to his mother's and his father's very high fair complexion. He was actually better looking and did not need it.

My dad's vote of no confidence in me while I attended the University of Maryland and his rush to get me in the Vietnam War was painful. However, a strength in me came from somewhere during the semesters that followed my exemption for the selective service. Some anxiety and pressure was dismissed from my mind, not having to worry every semester about my grades and the war. I got serious about growing up and preparing to honor my dad's wish to "break my plate." I reached that point and was ready to get my demonstration on the road.

I earned the necessary credits for graduation in summer of 1970. I was on the Dean's List for the final three semesters. I did not march at the commencement exercises. I was twenty-three years old. I was tired and worn trying to grow up, transcending academic standards between segregated and white schools, being a mother's boy, being gay, and figuring out how to move out on my own.

It was past time for me to be a man. I was happy to graduate, but I felt no sense of victory as far as my dad was concerned. He still considered me dumb and lucky. I still had a lot of work to do to be grown and independent and, most of all, allow my dad to break a plate. Those college years were a good ride, and I never really knew how good they were until I had to make it on my own. I was happy in spite of everything, but now equally as ready to say good riddance to him too.

Thank God the echo of my mother's words resonated in my head from the time I found a way to get my driver's license: "Never let someone tell you what you cannot do. You figure a way to get what you want done on your own. Learn to standup on your own two feet." Throughout my life, I never stopped thanking my mother for sticking with me during my difficult growth process to manhood and independence and paying my tuition for college, which was a fortune for her. She would reply, "Stop thanking me, boy! That is what mothers are supposed to do if they have the money, and you did the work." What could I say; I just loved and admired her more and more.

I returned home after my college graduation. I landed a job within two weeks in my field, and I was earning $7,200 per year. My dad thought that was a huge amount of money. I did not. I thought I was underpaid; however, if I were wise, I had better get a job immediately to please my dad. When my dad entered the workforce as an adult, he was working at the Alcazar Social Club during the 1930s. He was earning $7 per week, seven days a week. I had a college degree from a white institution, but the question for me was, who was going to hire me in the white marketplace and pay me a salary commensurate with my education and inexperience? The University of Maryland Placement Office offered me a job selling life insurance door to door, on commission. My college within the university was Family and Consumer Sciences. I did not accept the job, so I was on my own. The job offer from the university placement office didn't even make sense, considering my major. My dad's attitude was "You take what you can get." That is what he did for thirty years. I thought I was a different breed, but I had my feet under "his" dining table, and the plate was not broken yet. I settled for what I could get in the shortest period of time.

I could see when I returned home that my parents had changed their lifestyle. My moving back home was cramping their new style of living. They had spread out all over the house. They each took separate bedrooms; my dad enhanced his man cave in the basement, and my bedroom had been turned into a study for my mother and her worldwide stamp collection. My dad had started hanging his clothes in my bedroom closet. The University of Maryland ride was over. Needing to move back home was a dreadful thought for them, and for me as well.

Confronting their new life forced me to see that I needed to move on for myself and for them very quickly, ASAP! I resumed some of my high school chores out of respect. After having five years of freedom at no cost to me, the change was dramatic. I was twenty-three years old, six foot three inches tall, wearing a size 13 shoe, and sporting a large afro. I felt ridiculous living at home. I certainly did not want to start cutting the grass again, but I didn't want to see my father cut it. He had the money to hire someone to cut it but would not pay. In my eyes, my parents had aged. I did not remember the gray hair and the slower movements on a regular basis. It was heart-wrenching to see. I felt in a small way responsible.

My dad made me pay minimal rent. I saved my money to buy a car and to move out on my own. I started buying basic things in preparation for an apartment just as my mother had, years earlier when building the family house. My dad didn't need my rent money, but he enjoyed having the extra money just to blow. He was truly happy to take the money from me. I was happy to give it to him. It was more than fair after the years of sacrifices my parents made for me all through birth, puberty, teen, and college years. They taught independence to all their children from day one. They called it "I can't wait to break a plate." My plate, the third plate, the last plate was in rapid process of being broken.

Within six months, I purchased a new car and made a security deposit on an apartment. My dad wanted me to stay at home a little longer so I could pay cash for my car, but I was in a hurry to get out on my own at the earliest possible date. He and my mother never owned a substantial car until 1964. It was a black Buick Skylark with a baby-blue interior—the prettiest car he ever owned. But El Cheapo (my name for my dad) would not pay extra for air-conditioning or power steering, which did not make any sense to me at all; but this was my dad. Driving this beautiful car was like driving a Mack Truck without the power steering. My parents still owned that car when I returned home from college in 1970. I purchased a new 1971 Volkswagen Super Beetle. The color was shantung. It was beautiful to me, and I was happily on my way to being on my own.

Although my dad had preached breaking the plate to me and my siblings as a lesson to grow up and not be a burden on anyone, especially society, he was sad to see me go. I did not understand, and I was too euphoric with the thought of being on my own that I did not contemplate or consider what was going on in his head. I was celebrating the plate being broken. When I was all packed, extending my overjoyed good-byes to both of my parents, it seemed a little sad to both of them, but my dad's sadness stood out the most to me. My mother was sad because I was her baby and she had watched me struggle through to this point in life, but she was proud too. I wanted my dad to be happy for me, not sad. Their last child was driving away from home for the last time as a resident.

My dad asked, "Are you sure you don't you want to stay here a little longer to save a little more money?"

His comment was kind, but I was once again conflicted in that this was the day I thought he dreamed of; he was in a small way taking away some of my joy.

My dad was satisfied after he saw that all the money spent on my college education had paid off and, most of all, that I proved to him that I could support myself. This was what my parents expected from all their children. "Learn to take care of yourself!" is what they would say. I could have stayed on, but my lifestyle had changed too. I still had not revealed to them that I was gay, and I wanted to come out in my safe space. I did not think being at home would have been a good place to come out.

I was young, college educated, and the life lessons he taught me were beginning to penetrate. I was feeling guilty living off of my parents for so long. My siblings left home in their late teens. I was the last one to leave, and I stayed the longest. I was twenty-three. I needed to move on so they could enjoy whatever life they had left. When I reflect on my life, I could see my parents spoiled me beyond my belief. I really was privileged. I never felt poor a day in my life, unlike my parents said they were. They accomplished plenty and raised a family too. I knew from their experience that I could never have done the job they succeeded in doing with three children who were not a day at the beach!

As I gleefully drove across US Route 1 to Interstate 695, my gleefulness turned to a slight panic. I was on my own; I was responsible for me. After moving, I proceeded to furnish my apartment. After one year, I managed to get in debt. I worked up to four jobs at one time to retain the lifestyle my parents provided for me for twenty-three years. It was hard. One full-time job with the Baltimore City Public School System and part-time jobs at Morgan State University, Harford Community College, Baltimore

County Schools Evening Programs. I was young and had the energy to juggle it all. I applied and was accepted to Graduate School at the Johns Hopkins University and Loyola University of Maryland. I took getting ahead seriously and swiftly learned that I had squandered a lot of time in high school and college. I was single and wanted my parents to be proud of me, but this was going to take much time, money, energy, and education than I was aware.

My dad's continuous sense of humor and jokes finally paid off for him in a constructive way. After being invited to join Toastmasters International, Gunpowder Club 2562-18, my dad became enthusiastically engaged with the club's mission and its members. He enjoyed listening and learning how to deliver prolific speeches. Like everything he set his mind to do, he did it well.

Toastmasters began as a series of speaking clubs organized by Ralph C. Smedley during his time working for the YMCA in Bloomington, Illinois. The first unofficial Toastmasters meeting was held on March 24, 1905. Participants took turns leading and speaking at the club meetings; more experienced men evaluated short speeches. In 1970, Toastmaster's admitted its first female, Helen Blanchard, under the name of Homer Blanchard. In 1973, Toastmaster's International officially admitted women, and in 1985, Helen became the first female international president.

In 1970, not long after joining this group, he entered a humorous speech contest. He was awarded the highest honor in the club's humorous speech category. My dad had a sense of humor his whole life. Toastmaster's was the perfect venue for him to show his talent and get recognition. My siblings learned to be humorous through exposure to our dad. I never liked comedians or comics. They often made fun of and/or ridiculed others. I especially didn't like the jokes about Blacks and gays, considering I was both. He liked this kind of activity more than his high-paying job. However, as a Negro, he would have never earned the same money doing this kind of work as he did for the federal government. I am happy he chose to take care of his family.

The Department of the Army continued to send my dad to training up to his twenty-ninth year of federal service. As of 1970, my dad completed and received a Certificate of Training in the Chemical Biology Surety Program Course for Supervisors. The course entailed accident and incident control plans, chemical agents, personal protection, decontamination, toxic exposure first aid, and safety criteria. The course was given at Edgewood Arsenal, with George W. Connell, colonel, commanding.

When my dad first saw my apartment, he was shocked that I had obligated myself to a two-bedroom fully equipped unit. He thought the apartment was too much and too expensive for one person. He was a conservator of money; he thought that I was wasting money. He commented to my mother, "We never had anything like this when we were young." I was not in competition with him; I just liked what I liked, but yes, from a sensible perspective and an adult perspective, he was correct about my spending too much and being in debt.

By this time, gin had become a part of my dad's permanent identity. I had discretionary money to stock gin in my apartment for his visits. I upgraded my dad from Gordon's gin to more expensive Tanqueray. He was always pleased with this gesture. He was happy to be thought of and considered. Overall, he was a self-sacrificing man and very easy to please. My dad required little.

Drinking gin was yet another lost opportunity for us to bond for I never cultivated a taste for gin. Thus, he drank gin alone while my mother and I had a scotch and water. He quieted down about my apartment after a few sips of gin, but shook his head in amazement at how expensively I chose to live. I did not mention my debt, but he sensed it. I thought my apartment would make him happy for me.

My dad was never sure how I came to a conclusion. My choices never made sense to him. If I had any good fortune, he just called me dumb and lucky, as was the case when I finished college. He waited for my luck to run out, because before long, he knew I was doomed to fail. He simply did not see me as having that much on the ball. I had my mother's methods of survival, but he didn't think she made sense either. My mother and I were our own team and supported each other.

I too sometimes wondered how I made my decisions. I did not have a strategic plan. Simply, I was like my mother. I was materialistic, and my dad was not.

My dad had this philosophy that if you don't want anything, you can't be controlled. He felt that as long as you were obliged to someone or an institution, whether for a house or a car, you were being controlled. I thought control was in the head of another person. I had read in Eleanor Roosevelt's biography by Blanche Wiesen Cook that Mrs. Roosevelt's thinking was, "A slave is only a slave if the person agrees." I was like my mother, who always carried revolving credit, but she paid on time each month. My mother would bellow in explanation to my dad for her spending, "What is the point of living, Ros, if you can't get what you want every once in a while!" From our first Tappan Range, Frigidaire refrigerator, and Duncan Phyfe home furnishings, my mother always maintained an outstanding credit record.

I never felt stupid, or dumb and lucky as my dad called me. I lived my life by getting what I wanted. I did not feel controlled; and if I was being controlled, I agreed.

When my dad thought he was controlling me as a child, I did not feel controlled. I was obedient as he required, but I did not feel controlled. My mother had an expression: "You run your mouth and let me run my business." That was going on in my head as well: *Just let me run my business. You stay in your lane, and I will stay in my lane.*

My dad was schooled and worked in strict environments—the Catholic Church and the army. He felt that he was being controlled because he believed everything he was taught in the church and the military as the gospel truth. I never believed everything I was told. I don't think anyone who feels controlled is a happy person. I was happy going my jolly way. I took all the consequences that came my way, and many of my consequences were extremely tough.

In complete astonishment, my dad would say to my mother throughout my adult years, "That boy continues to do whatever he wants!" He could not understand me. He thought I was getting away with murder by not following rules absolutely. I followed the rules, but I did not believe in the whole rule. I, most assuredly, never fell for all the self-sacrificing rules of the Catholic Church. They changed the rules when it benefitted the church. I thought you needed to adapt rules to your personal circumstances. One rule does not fit all. It is your life. Not the church's life or the army's life. My dad followed the rules absolutely. This was why we bumped heads for years.

My mother didn't believe in a lot of man-made rules either. I seem to always be influenced my mother's camp. However, at times my mother thought I was a little extreme. She would say to me, "I don't know whose child you are. Your parents grew up poor. They struggled for a long time when they got married."

I witnessed my parents climb the socioeconomic ladder. I saw and felt their upward mobility and magnificent achievements. They worked hard.

Of Time and Spirit

I reaped and benefitted from their hard work and efforts. As a result, I was never poor. My parents were just as successful as any other parents in the world in my eyes. Furthermore, my parents accomplished under the opposition of oppression, prejudice, segregation, and racism, thus I give them tons of credit.

I learned from my father to follow rules, but I learned to consolidate the rules of mothers, who also needed to be herself. I would laugh when my mother would tell my father, "Ros, you don't know what you are talking about!" My mother had her own voice. My mother did not believe everything my dad said. She would tell me that I got the best of both parents. I did.

In 1971, my dad suffered a severe heart attack. After several months of recuperation, the doctors released my dad, stating he was in great shape and could return to work. Instead, he decided to apply for a disability retirement with thirty-one years of federal service. My mother thought he should work longer, but this was his opportunity to search for and find himself, his inner peace. With his many accomplishments and mounds of support from the Chemical Center at Edgewood, he had not discovered his personal happiness.

At my dad's retirement, the Department of the Army celebrated him in grand military style. They gave him a luncheon with many colleagues and friends. He received certificates for his thirty years of service, given only on decade anniversaries; a certificate of appreciation; and another certificate for his calculated thirty-one years of service on his official retirement date. In his remarks to his guest, he thanked everyone. He said he was happy to get out of the government. He wanted to do something different. He did not know what that would be, but he would look around.

After years of the internal torment of Catholicism, his first move was to join the Ames United Methodist Church in Bel Air. Catholicism was ingrained in him; the change was difficult. His mother, who was devout Catholic, probably would not have agreed with his change, but she was by this time deceased.

My mother never liked the Catholic Church from the beginning of her marriage to my dad. When she married my dad, she had to vow to raise any children born to the marriage Catholic. She did, but she regretted it. She did not feel her children had gained good religious training in the Catholic Church's Sunday Masses, in that the masses were spoken in Latin. My

115

mother did not understand Latin, so she felt there was little need to attend church: if you didn't know what was being said, nothing was gained.

Just as soon as I was eighteen, she felt she had discharged her responsibility to the Catholic Church and her mother-in-law. She independently joined Ames United Methodist Church, giving my dad freedom to remain Catholic. Methodist was her birth and childhood religion, and she was going back to her home Christian denomination. She had had enough of the Catholic Church, its segregation and hypocritical positions. My dad finally got the courage to make a change with a little coaching from my mother. He liked Ames, and the Ames congregation liked him. Soon, thereafter, he joined.

The beginning of his disenfranchisement in the Catholic Church germinated while serving in the military. It progressed over the years. The Catholic Church was segregated, and he tired of being seated in the choir loft of the Post Chapel and the back of the church at Saint Margaret's in Bel Air. His biggest reason for leaving the Catholic Church was because he was ostracized for asking questions about church laws. Catholic Church members and leaders saw my dad as a troublemaker, but they could not answer his questions about church inconsistencies.

I was living on my own during my dad's retirement years, I tried to include him in my life as I had included my mother all of my life. My dad never knew too much about me. He didn't know of my college friends, books that I read, or music I liked. He never knew that I suffered emotionally from his lack of approval of me. If I brought a girl home that I didn't show interest in, he would say to me, "What is wrong with her?" He wanted me to like just anybody. I was selective and particular, and he did not like that I was so choosy. It was still a struggle for us. We lived in our separate worlds.

I never recalled a time when my dad answered or talked on the telephone. He never wanted a telephone, just as he never wanted kitchen appliances or the home furnishing my mother purchased for the home. He complained when my mother had a telephone installed years earlier. On the rare occasion when he did pick up the telephone, I would say, "Hey, Dad! How are you doing today?"

He would reply, "I am doing OK. Well, here's your mother."

I thought, *Well, what is that?* To me, my dad was odd, and he liked being odd. My mother called him an odd ball.

116

During the beginning months of my dad's retirement, he attended the retirement parties of his former colleagues. He also started to make financial contributions to every charity that solicited him via US mail. I asked, "How do you decide which charity is your favorite?"

He said, "I just send two dollars to all of them." My dad had a stack of cancelled checks a foot high on the desk of his workstation. All his checks were made for two dollars to hundreds of charities. He kept every set of return address labels, notepads, pens, Christmas cards, calendars, flashlights, calculators, and certificates of support they sent him back as a thank-you. He kept everything! Most of it I considered junk.

My dad's visibility in Harford County had elevated over the years as a result of his community engagements. He eventually installed a private telephone line in his work area to enable volunteers and community leaders access to him. My mother and I kept the house telephone lines tied up for hours at a time. She and I were long winded according to my dad. We talked for hours on one call. My dad's callers could not get through to him. There was no such thing as call waiting.

Once in a while, I would call my dad on his private line. He would pick up and I would say, "Dad, how are you doing today?"

He would reply, "I am just sitting here looking natural." His reply was intended to generate some laughter or hilarity from me.

I would retort, "Then, stupid!"

He would chuckle, for he wanted this type of levity from me. I was uptight around him most of the time. We were the most uninteresting couple of men . . . father and son.

Coming out to my mother and my father was one of the hardest things that I ever did. Keeping my sexual orientation to myself was equally as hard. I did everything in my power to please my mother over my short life. We discussed everything, but I never told her that I was gay after I knew. She was the person who always told me that she never wanted to have me. I wanted to be wanted, and I knew to tell her I was gay was going to be heartbreaking for her. However, at age twenty-four, pretending to be straight for your mother is hard, and deceitful. I knew at four years old that I liked boys. I had carried this fact within me long enough. If it meant she disowned me, then it would be. I would live with my decision to come out alone.

My mother was a city girl from Washington DC. She was aware of gay men, but she called them sissies. Her father was the greatest influence in her mind-set. He ridiculed gay children and bullied his son, whom he thought was too close to his mother. My mother would say to me as a child, "You don't want to be like one of them, do you?"

In my mind, she saw my proclivities, and I was heading in that direction. She wanted to let me know that she didn't approve of her son being a sissy. She was imitating her father, who I thought was a hellion.

As I transitioned from my teen to young adult years, I was extroverted and well liked. I received lots of invitations to straight events, but internally, I was an outsider in that I did not expose my whole self. I was a loner watching boys making out, kissing, and having sex with girls. I was either sitting on the sidelines looking or walking around most venues trying not to look like a geek. In passing, the guys would check in with me and ask, "Are you having a good time?" I replied, "Yes!" In reality, I wanted to be necking like everyone else, but with a boy.

My mother and I talked by telephone several times a week even after I graduated college, especially on weekends. After I had attended my first gay party, I was so happy and so buoyant in our telephone conversation that my mother asked, "Well, who is she?"

I had to make a U-turn in the conversation. I was frustrated trying to cover up to please her. I was tired of hiding who I was.

I called my dad a few hours after my telephone conversation with my mother. I asked if he and my mother were both going to be home, because I had something to tell them. He said yes. I figured I would kill two birds with one stone—be truthful and get this over with without further concealment from me.

After arriving at our family home, I made all my normal jovialities and then with a strangled voice directly told my mother and my father that I was gay. My mother let out a cry of horror that magnified in my eardrums. She immediately started in with how it was not her fault. She took no responsibility. She did not want to be blamed or think she knew anything about my being gay. She said, "I breastfed all of my children. What did I do wrong? I tried as best I could to raise you to be a respectable young man. I tried to push you away from me."

On and on she cried as if I had been accused of committing the worse crime known to man. Watching her in such agony, I got tears in my eyes and tried to explain that it was not her fault. She did not do anything to me that was wrong—it was my biology. "But then how did you get this way? When I did everything I could . . .," she replied.

It was a dramatic scene. I felt bad for my mother. On the other hand, I felt relieved within myself to not have to keep up a pretense, a lie, to the two people who were my life support system.

It was my dad who finally opened his mouth and said in the most calming and soothing voice, "Zelma, Maurice has always been this way."

That was it! His voice implied, *How could you not know?* He ventured nothing more, nothing less. He had come to my rescue just like in the scene in *Mahogany* where Diana Ross modeled an originally designed dress that none of the fashion merchants bid on, when out of nowhere, a shout and a bid of ten thousand liras! Miss Ross was rescued and saved; I was rescued and saved. It was my dad who made my confession palatable. With my dad's approval, my mother was OK. He soothed her sense of guilt and took the responsibility away from her. She was cleared. I was cleared too.

Any insults, doubts, insecurities, or hurt feelings I felt from my dad over my short life were vanquished, conquered, and all wiped out. It was the first time I knew, without a doubt, that my dad loved me unconditionally. I was a mother's boy, but he was OK with me. He normalized me. I felt secure. I felt acceptable. He validated me as acceptable regardless of whether or not anybody else accepted me. I was his son with the simplest of words. He owned me, and I was no longer an outcast within myself. My self-assuredness was in place and firm. I could not ask for more; this was all I needed from my dad.

As society would have it, I endured a raft of hatred from the outside world for being gay, but I always knew within myself that my dad made the difference in my life on the day I was true to myself. He was waiting for me to decide who I was. He loved me unconditionally. My mother and my father were the only two people on earth I cared about who knew about my life choices. For the rest of the world, I did not care. I was free to be me. I was emancipated. As Stevie Wonder sang, "I AM HAPPIER THAN THE MORNING SUN..."

During 1973, one of my dad's coworkers at the Chemical Center was George Woods. George was not highly educated or a Christian believer to the extent of my dad in my opinion. George was not handsome to me. He wore thick eyeglasses. He drank often, and sometimes too much. He survived living in the "hood," and he looked like it to me. As I recall, he possessed a large vocabulary of profane words. He could be outspoken even when he was wrong. He was an, "I am going to set you straight" kind of man. He had a very kind heart and good intentions. His wife loved him dearly, and he loved her dearly in return; but in my opinion, he wasn't as bright as I saw my dad.

From my perspective, it was a privilege for George to associate with my dad. He saw my dad as respectable and smart and gave my dad lots of credit. At times, he joked and ridiculed my dad for being coolheaded and composed. I thought George liked my dad, and wanted to be somewhat like him. I thought his admiration was sincere, but my dad found him to be a little tedious to relate with because they did not have the same types of academic and cultural experiences.

George and his wife, Eleanor, decided to take a cruise after he retired. George and my dad retired from the Chemical Center a few years apart. George and Eleanor lived in Baltimore. Eleanor invited my mother and my dad to join them on the cruise. Eleanor and my mother were lifelong friends; this was how George came into my dad's life. When my mother approached my dad with the invitation, my dad flatly said, "No!" He did not want go. He forecasted the experience would be a disaster and he would be just asking for trouble if he accepted. Eleanor and my mother would have been just fine together, but he felt he would be obliged to keep George's company, and this he did not want to do for the duration of the cruise.

My mother didn't get into an argument with my dad, although she really wanted to go on the cruise to spend time with my dad and her girlfriend. They had been married for over thirty years, and she had learned to accept my dad as he was. My mother knew this was not the kind of activity that my dad would enjoy. A cruise sounded hoity-toity to my dad, and he did not like being around those types of people. This was a group tour, and my dad thought all the groups to be the same.

It had taken my mother years of fighting, coercion, and energy to get my dad to purchase their house and get it furnished. He resisted and battled in opposition for years too. An argument over a cruise was something she was not willing to take on. She replied to George and Eleanor's invitation with regrets.

When George received the negative reply to his invitation, he felt rejected. He knew he was less educated and less intellectual than my dad, and this made him feel that my dad was behaving as though he was better than George. He was insulted, and he called my dad all kinds of profane names by telephone. This was men locker room talk and normal for them. Essentially, he said to my dad, *You have worked all these years, and you are*

Of Time and Spirit

going on this cruise if it means I have to come to Forest Hill and pick you up. Furthermore, you need to take your wife out more. He hounded and annoyed my dad with his ravings until my dad relented just to get George off his back. My dad was not the type to engage in long and extended conflict with people, but George must have hit one of my dad's last nerves.

On July 28, 1973, the two couples sailed to the Caribbean via Holland America's *Rotterdam*. They embarked from New York City. My parents stayed with me in my Pikesville apartment the night before they were transported to New York. In the morning, I drove them to meet Eleanor, George, and the group being transported from Baltimore to New York for embarkation.

In my mother's excitement preparing for the cruise, she fell and broke her leg a week before the trip. This was something my dad had not planned. My dad was never a nurse. He hated being around sick people. Both of my parents were afraid of germs. My mother's broken leg in his mind translated to him needing to push my mother around in a wheelchair for the whole trip. This sickened his stomach and he said as much. He was pissed off. He composed himself, but he was frustrated with the thought. He did not want to go in the first place, and he could have murdered George for insisting he come along. When they returned home, my mother reported that my dad skipped many of the ship's activities to go hiking with the native people. I had never known my dad to hike; however, I am sure he wanted to escape the whole charade. My dad hated the experience, and this was the first and last cruise my parents ever shared.

121

CHAPTER 9

Freedom and My Dad's Discovery of Himself

1974

While a member of Toastmasters, my dad met a man named Mel McGee. Mel asked my dad to work with him and Derse Jackson to plan a National Advancement of Colored People (NAACP) picnic. My dad said he would work with the chapter. He reported that they all worked hard, but the turnout was not great, and they lost money on the event. My dad continued to work with the NAACP for the years that followed. African Americans were scattered throughout the county, and getting notices to all the families was difficult; moreover, the chapter was new and small, and the county was conservative, and many African Americans were afraid to be seen at the event.

By 1974, my dad had completed the Toastmasters Communications and Leadership Program. The club wanted my dad to assume a leadership role in their organization. He was trained and fulfilled all the requirements and became the administrative vice president for the club. He was honored, and the club was honored to have him.

The Bel Air Aegis featured my dad's appointment as administrative vice president for Toastmasters. In the article, they also mentioned his other community activities such as being PTA president at the Central Consolidated School, acting president of the Ross-Ruff Scholarship Fund, committee chair for Investments in the Vest Ten Investment Club, commander in the American Legion Post 55, member of the Ames United Methodist Church, and publicity chair for the Brotherhood of Man Gospel Choir. The article noted my dad's sustained interest in classical music, golfing, art, writing, and reading.

On August 26, 1974, Charles B. Anderson, Jr., county executive of Harford County, informed my dad he had been appointed to the Harford County board of directors. My dad was provided with an instrument of appointment, the membership list, and a copy of Section 230A of the Code of Public Laws for Harford County.

This was a big deal for my dad. Up to this point, his community service record reflected contributions to the black community. Harford County had remained segregated long after Civil Rights Legislation had passed in 1964. One year later, my dad composed and sent a letter to Mr. Anderson, resigning from the board.

Letter of Resignation from the Harford Center Board, July 2, 1975

Dear: M's Miller,

This letter is in reply to your letter and enclosed form of June 26, 1975. I am sorry that I was so slow answering, but I was trying to come to a decision, which was difficult to make. I feel that I have made the right one.

It is with regret that I submit my resignation to the Harford Center Board. I am honored that I was asked to serve.

The meetings I attended were of great interest to me, but mostly over my head. I could contribute very little in the majority of areas under discussion. My fields of endeavor were too far removed from the activities discussed, and my background too weak to be part of the decision-making body.

I gained much more than I was able to give, and I thank you for that.

Very Sincerely,
James R. Dorsey, Sr.

The Harford Center Board of Directors replied to my dad's letter on July 8, 1975, with a letter of regret. I thought: What integrity my dad had to resign from a position that he thought he could not contribute to. This could have been a prestigious role for him in the Harford County Government. It was like my dad to do what he felt was correct.

My dad read an article in the *Washington Post* that Cortez W. Peters, Jr., had died. My dad was somewhat taken aback. He had taken typing and shorthand classes there after completing high school. He was familiar with the outstanding works of both the father and the son. Cortez Peters was one of the few black-owned private schools in the nation and offered young blacks, especially those from the rural South, an entrance into the white-collar world. In the years that followed his death, DC mayor Sharon Pratt Kelly proclaimed May 23, 1991, as Cortez W. Peters, Jr., Day.

The Ames United Methodist Church continued to welcome my dad after he no longer attended the Catholic Church. Ames recruited him to participate in many of the church-sponsored activities. The United Methodist Church Conference enrolled my dad in their Lay Speakers Certificate Program. He met all the requirements and was recognized as a certified lay speaker for the Methodist Church, conference year 1974. The public-speaking skills that my dad acquired serving as club member of Toastmaster's International helped to bridge his expanded relationship with The United Methodist Church.

In June of 1975, my dad received a letter from Dr. Percy V. Williams, assistant state superintendent of the Maryland Public Schools, Division of Compensatory, Urban, and Supplement Programs (James A. Sensenbaugh was state superintendent). The letter was to thank my dad for the leadership he provided in planning and executing a homecoming day in honor of Dr. Williams.

Dr. Williams was the principal of the segregated Central Consolidated School for many years. Central was one of the two segregated public schools in the county for Negro children. It was located in the southern part of the county. Grades 1 through 12 were taught in this one physical plant. When the school was finally closed, the teachers, parents, and students hosted a celebration in honor of Dr. Williams for his leadership in operating the school during very difficult years for Negros everywhere. Students attended in droves to celebrate the recognition of Dr. Williams's distinguished career.

Of Time and Spirit

Dr. Williams acknowledged my dad's leadership as president of the PTA and the Ruff-Ross Scholarship Fund— which rewarded and aided college-bound Negro students.

At the Harford County Board of Education meeting held April on 12, 1977, my dad made the boldest move I ever remember. Harford County was extremely conservative, segregated, and racist. Housing, schools, restaurants, motels, and retail stores were all segregated. I remember when the Klu Klux Klan marched down US Route 1, very near our home. The county allowed the march to continue without a negative word of upset or rejection recorded. The county stated it was their freedom of speech. Negro residents were advised to stay home and pull the shades down in their homes. Can you believe my family and others walked around their homes in the dark in fear of the KKK in 1977?

My dad testified that over a period of years, he observed a pattern of racial discrimination in the school system. He said, "The Concerned Citizens believed there is an element of racism in the system and cited the small number of black educators in the schools who held positions at the principal level or above." He added that it took ten years for the schools in Harford County to completely integrate. He urged the Board to put quality in the schools "first and foremost."

In this setting, it took plenty of gusts for my dad to present this testimony in Harford County. The consequences could have been severe. He was retired from the federal government. The *Brown v. the Board of Education* Supreme Court ruling had been decided, and the Civil Rights Act of 1964 had been passed. These provided my dad with some leverage and protection. With all of the past legislation, my dad or his family could have experienced covert repercussions. His testimony was heard and acted upon. It proved useful within a short period. Leadership positions for African Americans were filled with speed. My dad was hailed a hero by many of the black teachers and the black Church for his taking the lead in another step toward equality.

Still not sure of his direction in life and still seeking something that really interested him, my dad enrolled in the H&R Block Basic Income Tax Course. He passed the test and met all the requirements on December 15, 1977. After completing the course, he worked with them for a short period of time but still had a sense of emptiness. He kept searching. What he said he learned most was, "It is better to just pay your taxes because to avoid paying them held heavy penalties."

Maurice W. Dorsey

December 8, 1978, my dad wrote the following note:

> Visited Edgewood Arsenal to see Joe Lawson a former colleague. Still working after 38 years there, I finished up 31 years in 1972. Joe's building was locked so, I went next door to ask about him. The people looked at me blank. Then I asked did they know any of the bosses, they didn't know anybody. While driving on post, I looked over all the old buildings I'd worked, and thought of all the old times and old guys. It seemed like everyone knew everyone else after they'd been there a short time. I guess I was disappointed because they didn't know me either. I was glad to leave. I could feel no sense of having ever belonged.

After thirty-one years of working, all the training and travel, all the awards, plaques, and certificates, no one knew my dad. Needless to say, no statue was elected in his honor.

On February 17, 1981, Maryland State governor Harry Hughes appointed my dad to the Harford County Property Tax Assessment Board to fill the remainder of the term of Norma Reeves. The governor explained that my dad's commission on the board had been forwarded to the Circuit Court in Bel Air, where he was to appear and qualify within thirty days as required by law. The shingle read, "Having trust and confidence in your integrity, prudence and ability." This was a lift for my dad, yet another recognition from the state level of government. He had both local, county, and state recognition visibility. This was not a poor résumé for a black man in Harford County. He was a big wheel, as I saw from my eyes.

On March 12, 1981, the *Aegis*, printed an article that stated, "Mr. Dorsey came in here one day and said he had been over at the Courthouse being sworn in." The Tax Appeal Board appeared not to know at that time that the governor of the state had appointed my dad to the board. There must have been some behind-the-scenes work going on here. In that Harford County, officials had not made this move on their own accord. My dad's reputation must have been more far reaching than the county government.

On July 6, 1983, Governor Hughes reappointed my dad to the Harford County Property Tax Assessment Appeal Board for a term of five years. The letter also read, "It gives me great pleasure to reappoint you because I recognize the valuable services you have already rendered the State and its people and I am confident that you will continue your unselfish devotion to the public interest." A truer statement about my dad had never been written. The *Aegis* printed in both the June 9, 1983, and July 14, 1983, issues of their newspaper that my dad was the first ever black to sit on the board. This was astounding to the African Americans in Harford County, who showed the greatest admiration for my dad.

The United Methodist Church, Baltimore East District School of Discipleship, noticed my dad's statewide recognition. He was recruited to the Advance Lay Speaker Program and received a certificate of completion in October 1983 from Richard Hogue, dean, and Charles E. Wolfe, instructor. My dad was preaching up a storm in the Methodist Church with the reserve of a Catholic priest.

I was well into my thirties when my dad told me the most horrifying story of his life. The story of the death of his baby sister Rosalie. On one of my many Saturday visits with my mother and my father, my dad was sipping a gin and orange juice, and he began to tell me about his baby sister Rosalie. Of all the family stories I had heard over almost forty years, I had never heard this story.

He began the story of his baby sister Rosalie who loved him to death. She would cry when he left for school in the mornings. As a baby, she crawled on the floor, and she would grab my dad's pants legs, imploring him to pick her up. My dad, would lift his baby sister and play with her for a while but then had to depart for school. She loved him, and he loved her with all his heart, he said. "She was cute and innocent," he said. Rosalie treated my dad as her father when he was a brother.

My dad was the second oldest boy. She was the baby of the seven living children. He too was a child from my perspective.

On the day of this story, my grandmother informed my dad as he was playing marbles in their backyard that she was leaving the house. She told him to keep an eye on things. She said to listen for Rosalie, that she was napping.

What my dad did not know was that his mother had left a pot of white potatoes cooking under a low heat in the kitchen to be used for the potato salad she was making upon her return. She had only run to the corner store for some mayonnaise. She was hosting a birthday party for herself that evening.

He explained to me that he did not know the water had evaporated from the pot of potatoes. Subsequently, the pot caught fire, and the house burned down, killing his baby sister Rosalie. I was absolutely horrified for my dad and his sister.

My dad began to cry as he told me this story. It was the most horrible story that I had ever heard. I was shocked to see my father cry. I shouted, "YOU KNOW IT WASN'T YOUR FAULT, DON'T YOU?"

As he relived the story, he was grief stricken. He looked at me with tears in his eyes and said, "Ma never said." He wiped his eyes with a white handkerchief and cried more.

I was absolutely paralyzed by this story and to see my dad in this state of pain. I had no idea as his son or a human being how to console my dad. I stated again, "DADDY! IT WAS NOT YOUR FAULT! YOU KNOW IT WAS NOT YOUR FAULT, DON'T YOU? YOU WERE A KID!" I was not liking my grandmother for one minute at this moment, not caring that she must have been in pain too.

All these years, my dad had pinned up in himself that he was responsible for his baby sister's death. It was no wonder to me now why he was drinking gin and searching for inner peace. My telling him that it was not his fault seemed to eradicate and relieve a lifetime of his guilt. He dried his eyes with his handkerchief and took another sip of his gin. My nerves had tightened, and I was stiff. My mother was silent. I had never heard of such a story ever and was shocked that my mother and I, as close as we were, never told me this story.

From that moment forward, I consciously and deliberately tried to make up for all the love he never felt from his mother. His story and his reaction sank me. I could not imagine a person living with this amount of sorrow all their life. I was going to love him up for the rest of his life, and I did. It is amazing how selfless he was and how selfish I was as a child, never knowing his inner story.

In 1983, my dad was the first recipient of the Ames United Methodist Church's George B. Gwynn Christian Service Award. My mother was asked to write his biography.

In the biography she wrote for the church, she included something that many people did not know. Back in 1975, my dad was introduced to an elderly African American lady from the county who was functionally illiterate. She had been a maid for one of the wealthier white families in the county. When the patriarch of the family died, my dad was asked by the children if he would take over the duties of attending to the elderly

Of Time and Spirit

lady's finances and transportation needs. They no longer had a need for her. She was able to live independently and care for herself but did not know how to count money nor could she drive an automobile. My dad's flawless, law-abiding reputation was strong and widespread in the county. My dad accepted and performed this daunting request for over a decade. They paid my dad nothing to do this.

I knew of this lady and the stress, at times, that she caused my dad due to her illiteracy and advancing age. I have never heard of another human being on the planet taking care of a non-relative for a total of over eighteen years until she died. My dad was a saint in my judgment, and everyone else who knew of this arrangement thought so as well. This was one of the highest compliments my mother gave my dad during their marriage.

My dad wrote in a note on September 6, 1985,

> *"I am my own psychiatrist. What to do? I can holler but I can't sing. I am on the Ames choir, not by choice; some year ago. I was practically forced in over my own objections. Now I am in there hollering in bass, tenor, alto, and soprano, all in a single song. There is now a drive for a really good choir. I was uncomfortable before. Now I am miserable. The men's chorus was not quite so choosy either. We sang and had fun. Most of us were untrained. Now there is a new brand of singer coming in. They're good. They outwardly show contempt for the hollers like me. The old timer's say, stay-in."*

My sister became interested in family genealogy. She started asking my dad a lot of questions about his family. My sister had published articles nationally and in Baltimore's local papers. I was so proud of her; I would matte, frame, and display her newspaper and magazine articles. I always loved those members who added strength to our family. She continued to be a star.

As she was doing her research, she asked my dad if, in his spare time, he would do some research for her on his family. He did, and it was pure "Magic!" for him. In this one request, my dad found the missing key to his life. He discovered his passion in life: *researching Negro history.* My sister's request was unknowingly a life gift to our dad. It had only been in recent years that Black history was accepted in the American canon, so it is no wonder why he had not discovered himself or this interest. He knew

129

nothing of where he came from. Subjects such as Black history were not in school curriculums, certainly not in the Catholic school or public schools he attended. Those institutions were all run by middle- and upper-middle-class white men. Then and now, much has yet to be written. My dad found his home, his passion, his love. He was at last contented and had found inner peace with this kind of work and his place in the world. It made sense to him; he got it.

Don Morrison from the Bel Air *Aegis* wrote a full article on my dad and his newly discovered interest in Black history. *"Ros' Dorsey helps complies history of blacks in Harford'* (May 15, 1986). My dad was sixty-seven years old. He was really upbeat about discovering Black history. He thought this was an area where he could accomplish good. The Harford County Historical Society found a space for my dad to work in the basement of the West Courtland Street facility. They gave him the title of curator of maps. On Thursday mornings each week, he rummaged through files of maps. In the evening, he would return to help catalogue a collection of literature on blacks and other minorities.

This was a big job, and my dad said that it may take the rest of his life to complete. At the time, the society had a collection of 20,000 maps and 10,000 volumes of books devoted to African American history. My dad said in Mr. Morrison's article that he enjoyed this work so much that he would like to retire from his work at the church to spend more time at the Society." He was a Sunday School Teacher at the church and elder.

From the beginning of his work at the Society, he was faithful to his Thursday morning cataloging of maps and evening book sorting. He was like Don Quixote as he first sang, "The Impossible Dream" from the 1965 Broadway musical *Man of La Mancha*. My dad was following his quest to find his passion. He was putting together the most extensive collection of maps in the region that would eventually be used by the general public. My dad called it "a labor of love."

In the winter issue of *Harford Historical Bulletin* (Number 27), my dad published an article: "Men at War, Edgewood Arsenal, Maryland 1918." The section of the article on Black Presence is from extracts from the General Roster of Edgewood Arsenal (November 1, 1918) demonstrated on a comparative basis. Only Company "B" and Company "F" are shown. When the United States entered World War I, no black men were allowed in the marines, coast guard, or the air force, and in the navy, they could only serve as mess men. During the war, the laborers and stevedore battalions were made up almost entirely of Negros, except for commanding officers.

Over 99 percent of the Negro officers and men of Edgewood Arsenal made an application for an opportunity to serve overseas. This opportunity was denied them; they felt their work on this side of the ocean was more important than their presence on the other side.

Up to 1986, my dad's mind was still taunted by the indoctrination of the Catholic Church. He entered in his journal on March 30, 1986,

> I had difficulty understanding why my dad would not leave the Presbyterian Church. Sundays, we went to ours (Catholic), he went to his. It was a puzzle to me how a Presbyterian could be as nice as Catholic. My dad was a good man. He worked hard, but we still didn't have much, but I thought everybody was that way. I didn't care because this life was temporary anyhow and I was certain of Heaven.

In his notes, he wrote a draft letter to my sister:

> I struggle over my articles. Nobody reads them. I have found through the years that just because I spent time on some project does not mean that all the world will appreciate. There are so many views (differing) on the same article you couldn't count them. As one man said: 'options are like noses, everyone has one. Another guy produced a play as he saw it, people stayed away in droves.' I was taught in the Catholic School that I was obliged to attend anything that the sisters and priests prepared, plus I must be on time. I carried this over into my worldly life. I was ashamed if I did not participate in everything. Most of the time I wound up doing the largest part of any project. Most people operate on CP time, the others don't show up and don't even call, much less acknowledge.

Communicating with my dad remained difficult for me, but I loved him with all my heart. We shared so little in common, but we continued over the years to reach out to each other. As we each got older, I wanted let him know that I loved him, but neither one of us had the communication skills to simply say, "I love you." Men in this era just didn't say things like this to other men.

Since verbal communications between us were not effective, I started writing him letters expressing years of appreciation for all he had done for me in my life. I awakened one morning, and in the miniscule period of time between sleep and waking that I call twilight, my intuition told me that of all the people in the world, my dad loved me most unconditionally. Once I was settled into my day, I sat at my desk and wrote a note to my dad to express to him what my intuition had said to me.

As I wrote this message to him, I felt that I was betraying my mother, who was my bedrock. I needed, however, to convey to my dad his importance in my life. What I was writing was true. Neither one of us had ever expressed feelings or emotions throughout our lives. We never had the slightest touch. When I see men today hugging, touching, loving their son in proud admiration, I cry because I never experienced touch or any form of affection from my dad.

It had been explained to me frequently as a child and a young adult in my attempts to figure out my dad that men of that generation did not communicate feelings and emotions. My dad's actions were that of a father, I understood, but I needed the verbal as well.

On November 10, 1987, he replied to my letter:

Thank You for your confidence, your intuition tells you right my love for you is unconditional. Dear Son, I appreciate your note more than you know. Over the years I guess I did not talk much to you about my feelings, but I was always aware of your aim for the higher goals in life. I have always been proud of you without expressing it. Unfortunately, that's a trait that I developed or inherited but inside I feel a great deal of love. On your last visit to the house we told jokes, and your laughter made me happy. So, remember, I love you unconditionally and stay happy!

Very Sincerely,
Dad

Of Time and Spirit

This short message touched my heart so deeply I had the message matted and framed on archival paper, and it hangs in my house today. To this day, I tear up when I reread this note. From here, we continued to write to each other.

My dad remained conflicted between his religion and his real-world experiences, although he had found his passion for Black history. In my dad's later years, he identified with television host Phil Donahue as a Catholic. Phillip John Donahue was the host of *The Phil Donahue Show*, later known as *Donahue*. It was the first talk show format that included audience participation. The show had a twenty-nine-year run on national television in America. He was called the "king of daytime talk." Oprah Winfrey has stated, "If it weren't for Phil Donahue, there would never have been an *Oprah Show*." My dad added a journal entry on March 30, 1987:

> Like Phil Donahue, I came up Catholic. I felt that anyone not of my faith would certainly go to hell. I became an altar boy, was confirmed. I missed many opportunities with anxious young women, because I thought it was a wrong to even embrace out of marriage. This way was hard. Masturbation was wrong. So, sex was out. I see this now as a handicap. Unnatural. I was like the modern born-again person is today. I can't stand them." "Church still a part of my life with guilt trips. Family and friends become born again. Something wrong with drinking, smoking, playing cards, celebrating holidays.

My dad remained active with the Harford County Chapter of the NAACP throughout the years of their progression. My sister, Margaret Pagan, writer, wrote a profile of my dad for the NAACP newsletter in October 1989. She wrote of my dad's betterment of life for Blacks in Harford County. She wrote that the foundation of many of his activities began while he was in Toastmasters International Club.

She acknowledged his contributions with the Ruff-Ross Scholarship Fund, Ames United Methodist Church, and his appointment to the Harford County Property Tax Appeals Board, the first black to ever hold this position. Moreover, after pursuing research in Afro American history, it overtook him. Working with other history buffs, researchers, and writers, he has published his findings in the *Harford Historical Society Bulletin*, and the *Flowers of the Forest*, a Black genealogical journal. He has exhibited in Ames United Methodist Church Fellowship Hall, the Harford County Historical Society Office, and the Harford Community College.

At some point, as my dad aged, he wrote another original poem, not dated:

> *Old Age is Hell by James Roswell Dorsey, Sr.*
> *The body gets stiff, you get cramps in your legs,*
> *Corns on your feet as big as hen's eggs.*
> *Gas in your stomach, elimination is poor,*
> *Take ex-lax at night, but still you're not sure.*
> *You soak in a tub or your body will smell.*
> *It's just like I said, "old age is hell."*
> *Teeth start decaying, eyesight is poor,*
> *Hair falling out all over the floor.*
> *Sex life is bad, it's a thing of the past,*
> *Don't kid yourself friends, even that doesn't last.*
> *Can't go to parties, don't dance anymore,*
> *Just putting it mildly, you're one hell of a bore.*
> *Liquor is out, can't take a chance, bladder is weak*
> *Might pee in your pants.*
> *Nothing to plan for, nothing to expect, just only the mailman*
> *With your social security check.*
> *So, if this holiday season you feel fairly well.*
> *Thank God you're alive, although old age is hell.*

On January 31, 1990, Ben Keenan wrote an article titled "Black History: Events, Programs Set to Note Social Impact." The article highlighted the events and programs for Black History Month in Harford County schools and libraries. He also mentioned those individuals who were setting up an exposition in the Harford Mall. Gwendolyn Hackley Austin made a short presentation followed by a question-and-answer session on local Black history with my dad, curator of maps for the Harford Historical Society at Aberdeen Library. My dad was honored to be invited and was one of the exhibitioners at the Harford Mall.

As my dad got older, he continued to write on scratch paper or pads to jot down his thoughts and feelings. He wrote this in 1991:

I am not a senior citizen. I am only seventy-two. I have come to this conclusion on the basis of my respect for my grandparents. They told me that wisdom comes with age. It may be that we live longer and it takes wisdom longer to get to us: I am still waiting.

I became aware of this fact recently. A storm with thunder and lightning hit the neighborhood and the electrical circuits in the neighborhood and my house went haywire. Eventually, all circuits came on except my central air. I checked all circuit breakers and switches with no success.

Then the humidity and heat returned full force. I called the air conditioner manufacturer and installer. They sent a repair person who in three minutes stated there was not current to the unit. I should call my local gas and electric company to get power restored and then called them back. They only repaired air conditioners that had power to operate them. They presented a bill for $36.95, which I calculated to mean I paid about $10.00 per minute for advice.

In celebration of Black History Month in 1995, the *Aegis* considered contributions of the Black church in Harford County for their February issue. They published my dad's most prolific article titled "Religion: Convictions Run Deep." By this time in my life, I had earned three graduate degrees and had never written anything that I thought compared. Here are some of the excerpts from his article:

Strong religious conventions have been imbedded in black Americans since the beginning of slavery. Under the deplorable conditions of slavery, husbands and wives were separated and sold into lives of servitude and babies were stolen from their mothers as soon as they were born. Blacks had virtually nothing to call their own, not even their own lives.

Denied their human rights, blacks clung to the one thing that would not be taken away from the —their faith in God, a faith that has held strong down through the years.

Worship services, usually held in secret, brought salvation, freeing blacks from the shackles of slavery, if only momentarily. The history of the church parallels the struggle of blacks.

In 1798, Harford County had two Episcopal churches, two chapels, two Presbyterian churches, one Catholic church, one Baptist church, six Methodist churches, and three Quaker meeting houses.

In 1810, the county had 4,431 slaves. The Watters Methodist Meeting House erected in 1773, and still standing, has a gallery where slaves worshiped.

Also, free blacks were seated in the gallery during services at the various churches.

In 1849, a small group of free blacks from Havre de Grace and the Gravel Hill area saw the need for a church of their own. They met at the home of James Peaco on Zion Hill and established a church, calling it Mount Zion Meeting House.

During one of the fellowship sessions, a discussion came up concerning Richard Allen, a black freeman who was pulled from his knees in a Methodist Episcopal Church.

Later, when some of the members heard of an AME Conference in Philadelphia, they attended its sessions. They like what they saw and heard. They joined and became Mt. Zion AME Church. In 1874, the original church was moved from Zion Hill to Green Street in Havre de Grace and renamed St. James AME in honor of Peaco.

In 1849, the conditions that existed in the Zion Hill area were repeated in the lower end of the county.

In Michaelsville, there was the Garrison Chapel Methodist Episcopal Church. Black people were allowed to sit in the gallery which had been built especially for them.

It is said that free blacks and slaves were allowed if their conduct and general deportment were proper. Feeling pressured, the blacks began meeting in different Christian homes. Eventually, they purchased a lot and materials and built their own Methodist Church on Old Post Road in Aberdeen.

Many changes occurred from the 1840's to the 1860's because of slavery. Abolitionist and anti-slavery groups formed. Six Southern states withdrew from the union and adopted a flag of their own, calling themselves the Confederate States of America.

Slaveholding Methodist formed their own conference. Two Harford County churches joined the United Methodist Church South. In 1861 Confederate forces bombed Fort Sumter and the Civil War began.

Blacks offered to enlist in the Union Army at their own expense. In 1863, the Emancipation Proclamation was signed. Thirty-eight thousand black soldiers died to save the Union . . .

. . . The Freedmens's Bureau was established in 1865 by an act of Congress. Its principal aim was the education of blacks, and funds were provided to build schoolhouses and pay teachers.

Three such schools were erected in Harford County in 1867, receiving most of its support from the bureau . . .

. . . the third, was the Mc Comas Institute, serving as a school, church hall and community meeting house . . .

. . . From the time, the freed slaves and their ancestors were given any liberties, the church took part. Foremost in their minds was education for their children and a house of worship for themselves.

A beacon of light in the community, the black church realizes the vital role it plays in people's lives. The church's mission carries

*it beyond the church doors, taking it out into the community
where it not only feeds hungry souls, but hungry mouths; where
it not only imparts spiritual wisdom, but academic*

The beauty and power of this article is that it encompasses my dad's whole life experiences from his beginning in the segregated Catholic Church, the segregation of the United States Army, and the segregation of the private and public schools he attended, to the streets where he was born and lived. At birth, an individual's foundations to living are set for most people, both black and white. From the beginning to the ending of the lives of slaves, coloreds, Negros, Blacks, and African Americans are all truncated by prejudice segregation, racism, and inequality.

My dad pretty much up chocked all the injustices of his life in this published article. For my dad's whole life, he was attempting to understand and contribute passionately to the betterment of mankind. The classical education that he had received had not been put to its best use performing the work he did for thirty-one years at the Chemical Center, essentially developing weapons to kill people. He had attempted to fit together the pieces of his world not knowing the depth of history that preceded him. Not knowing that churches also had slaveholding parishioners and 38,000 black soldiers died to save the union. He experienced as a Negro many barriers in his life. He never gave up on finding his place and passion in the world. I wonder what my dad's life would have been if he knew the history of his people and if he had not faced the atrocities of racism.

Interestingly, the injustices that my dad was born to and lived through were passed down to his children. They too experienced these types of inequities in their lives. The fight for equality continues today. My sister opened my dad's eyes to Black history with a simple request for help in researching my dad's family genealogy. An amazing twist of fate. I only wished that he could have lived to write his own story for I am sure it would have been a million times better than what I have constructed from his scratches on paper, personal journals, and life records.

In 1864, the federal government established the Freedmen's Bureau to serve the needs of people affected by the Civil War. One of the primary concerns was education. As a result, the McComas Institute was constructed in 1867. It was the third of three Freedmen schools established in Harford County.

Of Time and Spirit

In 1872, the McComas Institute was taken over by the Harford County Board of Education after the Freedmen's Bureau was abolished. The McComas Institute was officially closed in 1939. The Mount Zion Methodist Church took over the building and used it as their community hall.

When the Mount Zion Methodist Church was closed, a group of community members organized the McComas Institute Association. They petitioned the state legislature and had the McComas Institute declare a historical landmark.

In 1995, the building was restored by the Historical Society of Harford County, where my dad was curator of maps, and opened as a museum by the association. The dedication service was held on September 23, 1995, and my dad was secretary of the association during this time.

Many organizations and individuals supported the program. The twenty-three original alumni were recognized. Remarks were made by Wayne Lingham, McComas Association president; Christine Tolbert, Hosanna Freedman's School; state senator William Amoss; Dr. Percy V. Williams, former state superintendent; and Mary Henson Demby, 1931 alumnus and valedictorian.

My mother and my father placed an advertisement of support remembering their parents and my dad's two deceased brothers and one sister, Rosalie, who died in the house fire. My dad collected patron advertisement from his children, grandchildren, brothers, sisters, nieces, and nephews to support the program. It was the first remembrance of his sister Rosalie I had ever seen. My dad finally made peace in his soul with her death. I think I contributed to this peace.

During 1996, those who read or heard of my dad's articles celebrated him far and wide. The Zeta Phi Beta Sorority, Inc., Omicron Chi Zeta Chapter, and the Harford County Community presented my dad with an Official Citation for his dedicated service to the Harford County community. It was signed by each of the state senators and delegates of Harford County: Senator William H. Amoss, Senator David R. Craig, Delegate Rose Mary Hatem Bonsack, Delegate Donald C. Fry, Delegate James M Harkins, Delegate Nancy Jacobs, and Delegate Mary Louise Preis on October 27, 1996.

On this same date, Paris N. Glendening, governor of the State of Maryland and John T. Willis, secretary of state, presented my dad with the governor's citation in recognition of outstanding service to the community and the state in honor of your dedicated volunteer work and the numerous civic and humanitarian endeavors you have supported throughout the years, and as an expression of our admiration, gratitude, and sincere congratulations as you are honored by the Zeta Phi Beta Sorority, Inc., Omicron Chi Zeta Chapter.

On February 21, 1997, the Department of Veterans Affairs, Wilmington, Delaware, Vet Center presented my dad with a Certificate of Appreciation for his service to the country and in recognition of Black History Month.

By 1998, my dad was elected president of the McComas Institute Association, Incorporated. In their newsletter of March 1998, in the section "President's Message," he wrote,

I was impressed when I read an article by Somerset Maugham. It set me to thinking. I grew up I Baltimore City from the 1920's to the 1940's. I went to segregated schools, churches, movies, and stores. I resented the treatment, but my dad was afraid for his children, and ordered us to keep our mouths shut, which we did.

In the 1940's I got a job at Edgewood Arsenal. I had to ride a colored bus to work. On my job, I changed clothes in a colored locker room, and used the colored toilets. I still kept my mouth shut.

One day on the job, all bedlam broke loose. The radios were turned to high volume. Japan had dropped a bomb on Pearl Harbor, killing many soldiers and destroying many army planes. I felt at a time like this all Americans regardless of race, color, or creed should help; so, I enlisted. I was given an Army uniform and assigned to a colored barracks, with toilets marked for colored only.

After seventeen weeks of infantry basic training in Alabama, two weeks advanced infantry in Fort Meade, and thirteen weeks of combat training in Italy, I was ready for the frontline. Through all this I kept my mouth shut.

One day in my barracks, my name was called. I reported to the captain, who took me to headquarters. He had my school records. He asked me if I had attended Cortez Peters Business School. I told him I had. He gave me a handwritten letter, and told me to type it. I did and was promoted to Sergeant that same day.

As I look back, I thank my now deceased dad for telling me to keep my mouth shut. I thought of my dad when I read the words of W. Somerset Maugham. With age, you gain wisdom; then open your mouth.

In February 1999, Karen Toussaint of the *Aegis* staff wrote an article in the "I Get Around" section of the newspaper: "Take a trip back in time at the McComas Institute." She wrote,

Those who have interest in traveling back in time and visiting a genuine one-room schoolhouse can do so Saturday. At the same time, you can get a built-in history lesson, because the Mc Comas Institute on Singer Road in Joppa was built by the Bureau of Refugees, Freedmen and Abandoned Lands (Freedmen's Bureau) in 1867. The reason was to educate black youngsters, both those born free and newly-freed slaves, who had been forbidden to learn to read under laws called slave codes.

'The federal government supplied the materials and a teacher, and the community supplied the labor,' said James Dorsey, president of the Mc Comas Institute Association, the group which works to preserve the site as part of Harford history.

James R. Dorsey, Sr. is one of the guides who gives tours to the public on the third Saturday of each month from noon to 4:00 p.m.

My dad and I continued to write letters to each other over the years. I would take a gift of some kind to my parents on each visit just for fun. On one occasion, I took a generous check and a jumbo roll ten-pack of toilet tissue and presented it to my dad along with the comment: "Here is something for you to wipe your butt with!"

He laughed; he still liked jokes. During this visit, I shared with my mother and my father that I was changing jobs again. By this time, I had five full-time jobs and five part-time jobs. My dad looked and me and asked, "Maurice, why do you change jobs so much?"

I replied, "I don't know. I guess I never decided what I wanted to be when I grew up."

My response clicked in his mind. He replied, "Interesting, Maurice. I never knew what I wanted to do either." I was surprised that with all that he had done, he was not content with what he had been doing for years.

On March 24, 1999, at eighty years old my dad wrote the following thank-you letter to me; and as you read, you can discern his humor was still in play:

Dear Son

I briefly saw the very generous donation that you gave the family in the form of a nice check. I had the opportunity to place my signature on the back, in the presences of your mother who immediately retrieved it and headed for the mall. Nevertheless, I thank you for whatever your mother buys.

I assume you and Bob are doing well. I apologize to him, when he answered the phone I did not recognize his voice, and I abruptly asked for you without speaking, tell him I am sending a belated hello.

To me Maurice, this is a tough time. It seems that my whole lifestyle will be changed. I have visited these senior citizen homes, and to me they seem dull and sad. I hope at least they have buses to the Casino, and a place to obtain gin.

I have started to ramble but the purpose of this letter was to thank you for your generosity and thoughtfulness. I am sure that the good Lord will bless you! Mother and I greatly appreciate your thoughtfulness.

Thank you so much, Dad loves you

Of Time and Spirit

For my dad and me, it took almost a lifetime for us to write or say the word *love*. But before he passed away, we were pretty fluid in love without being mushy toward each other. We were finally content with each other.

On April 21, 2000, my dad received a letter from the Historic Preservation Commission c/o the Harford County Department of Planning and Zoning. Christopher Weeks, historic preservationist, wrote in the letter that the commission had unanimously voted to present him with the 2000 Historic Society Preservationist Award for his countless volunteer hours working with the Historical Society of Harford County and his great contributions in celebrating the county's African American heritage.

James M. Harkins, Harford County executive, and W. Paul Thompson, Jr., chair of the Historic Preservation Commission, added to the award inscription: Private preservation groups depend on volunteers to survive. The Historical Society of Harford County, Maryland's oldest county historical society, was lucky that James Dorsey, Sr., was around. He single-handedly organized the Society's extensive (but chaotic) map collection; he answered thousands of researchers' request for assistance; he subtly kept his (sometimes overly opinionated) co-volunteers working together smoothly; he helped secure state funding to restore Harford's two Freedmen's schools; and he led tours of Edgewood Arsenal and other historic sites. And he did it all with a smile on his lips and a twinkle in his eyes.

My dad had turned eighty-one years old this same month the award was presented. His health had begun to deteriorate. He could not attend the breakfast award ceremony at the Liriodendron in Bel Air. My sister, appropriately so, accepted the award for our dad.

My dad and my mother had moved to Owings Mills, Maryland, to be closer to their children. My dad needed far more care than my mother and the family could provide. My dad had dementia, cardiomyopathy, congestive heart failure, hypothyroidism, and chronic renal insufficiency.

My mother and I searched almost every nursing home in Baltimore City to find the very best one for my dad. It was a struggle because most were crowded and understaffed. A few smelled unsanitary. My dad had not been a resident of the city in over sixty years, thus his case was not given priority.

The Veterans Medical Center on Loch Raven Boulevard eventually found an opening with the help of a former classmate of my sister's. After reviewing my dad's military records and saw that he had served in World War II, he was accepted to the Rehabilitation and Extended Care Center. It was one of the happiest days of my mother's life. She was exhausted, and I was not far behind.

On May 19, 2000, Karen Toussaint, *Aegis* staff writer who had followed my dad's volunteer work, wrote an article, "Harford Residents Preserve History, Natural Beauty." She highlighted the work of the honorees of the Historic Preservation Awards Ceremony. There was a picture accompanying the article with my sister on the front row with a happy smile holding my dad's award.

My dad died on December 2, 2000. According to his death certificate, he died of a stroke. There were other contributing conditions but not the underlying cause.

My dad's funeral was held on December 6, 2000, at the Ames United Methodist Church. My mother and I raced to make the final arrangements. As with my dad's two heart attacks, I never felt of greater use in my life than to work with my mother on my dad's final arrangements. It was a beautiful one-hour service. There was an opening hymn, presented by Reverend Eric W. King, Sr.

Reverend King spoke of the many deeds of my dad's life, his marriage, children, career, and community. He focused mostly on my dad's talents and unlimited time servicing the church, not only for him, as the current pastor, but for each pastor that presided over the church. He talked of my dad as Sunday school teacher for the junior and senior classes, designing the church replica that hangs in the sanctuary, my dad's singing in the senior choir, writing the church history and keeping it updated, and his organization of Black history displays.

Reverend King went on to say that there was little that went on in the church that my dad was not involved with, and no chore was asked of him that he did not accomplish. My dad was a loyal member of the Finance Committee and the Vision Committee. He kept the attendance and dues records for the choir, the Bible study, and Sunday school dues. One year, he said, my dad wrote a Christmas play and regularly made monetary contributions to replenish the Christmas Fund. He said that my dad was often on his hands and knees under the podium fixing the electrical system. My dad was a trustee and a pillar of the church, just as he was marked on his Good Friday birthday.

My dad's life and his service were a gift to me. I recognized as I slowly matured to adulthood that I was privileged to have some of my dad's genes. Who could have ever asked for more in a father, especially when some children don't have a father at all, even when the father lives in the household?

The Historic Preservation Award was my dad's final public service award. It was symbolic of a crown that represented the passion of his public life: African American history.

He and my mother were married for sixty-two years. They are buried together in Bel Air Memorial Gardens. Their grave marker reads: "Together Forever." Their relationship endured all types of troubles; they were a team and transcended each and every challenge.

They sang from the same sheet of music when governing their children. They provided their children with advantages they, as children, never had.

My dad was not wealthy when he died, but he did not die broke. He said to me, "Maurice, I want you to see to it that I have a decent funeral." His knowing and acceptance of my close relationship with my mother he added, "Your mother will be in good shape." She lived very comfortably for another fifteen years after his death from his annuity, her annuity, the proceeds from the sale of the house my dad never wanted, and their years of savings. My mother had vision and foresight.

My dad said to me that he loved all his children. After they became adults, he said he never understood some of their life decisions. Each of his children participated in leisure time with my dad. My brother would visit Dad. They also took road trips to Atlantic City and Delaware Park. They shared libations together. My sister would visit my dad. They talked about books, writing, and Black history. As for me, I would visit my dad. He would sit quietly, with gin and orange juice in hand, and listen to my mother and me talk endlessly about things that were of no interest to him. He would say to us, "You all are not talking about anything." We all knew it, but it was a fun-time chatter, joy, and excitement. My dad and I continued to write letters to each other.

He had six grandchildren. He was generous to all of them, although it was my mother who doled out the gifts, usually cash, from the two of them. My dad was instrumental in helping one of his grandsons get employment. My dad awakened him for work each morning. My dad even made his breakfast and lunch as he sometimes did for me when I was a child.

After the funeral, some of the kindest words my dad used to describe me came from his county friends who made it a point to tell me what he said about me, words we never expressed face-to-face. The most important was: "I could count on Maurice." This was something I surely wanted him to know before he died, and he did.

EPILOGUE

My dad has been deceased for over twenty years. What remains for me are many gifts. His life from my lens is illuminating and immense. He led a life of learning, service, teaching, and leadership.

Although there was a twenty-eight-year difference in our ages, I learned that my dad and I were similar. I did not discern much of this until after he died. When I was young, many things about my dad were invisible.

We both had the experience of being baptized and confirmed, and we attended Sunday Mass in a segregated Catholic church. We each had huge struggles to untangle ourselves from man-made church laws and to find a home in our hearts to remain obedient to God. He was loved at the Ames United Methodist Church, and he never returned to the Catholic Church. I created for myself a personal relationship with God. My dad and I respected all religions, something he did not learn in Catholic school. My dad learned a lot in the Catholic school, but he believed too faithfully, and it also took a lot away from his life.

We both experienced the difficulty of being misunderstood by others. We both sought acceptance from our mothers. He wanted acceptance from his mother after his youngest sister died in the house fire, for which he felt responsible. I wanted acceptance from my mother because she repeatedly told me she never wanted to have me and I wanted to be wanted by her. The relationship between a mother and a child is primal; every child wants the love and acceptance of their mother. Perhaps this was the cause of my dysfunctional relationship with my dad, my need for my mother was greater, and perhaps my dad needed the acceptance of his mother more than me. At the very least, he had a great need to sedate himself with gin to soothe his inner pain, as I did with Scotch and water.

147

My dad and I valued education and continuously strived to get ahead in our respective careers. Our primary schools were segregated, and the quality of education we received was not equal to what white schools offered. Many of our dreams and aspirations were truncated by the dominant society. His by race, mine by race and sexual orientation.

We both worked in environments for approximately thirty years before we found satisfaction, contentment, and inner security and peace. We both strived for recognition and sought a place of contributing to humanity. His was the research and study of African American history; mine is yet to be determined, regardless we both persevered.

When my dad had his heart attacks, although he never wanted to have the surgery, I knew for sure that I was not ready for him to die. We both knew we had not completed our parent-child cycle. My dad was not perfect, and neither was I; but he was my hero, and he could always count on me.

In writing this summary, I needed to mature to understand the fears that my dad had for me, just as his dad had fears for him. I understand now why he had difficulty with my attending the Bel Air Senior High School, the University of Maryland, and living too large. He was afraid for me. Although I made it through difficult circumstances, as did he. He was correct as a father to have fears for his child.

What I have learned in writing about his life is that neither parents, education, marriage, children, career success, nor organized religion gives you inner peace. It is something that we find on our own, and it's not the same for everyone. This is why *The Razor's Edge* by W. Somerset Maugham was my dad's favorite book. He could identify with it. Although I did not choose the same favorite character he chose, he gave me his copy of the book before he sold the family house. He eventually understood and could see why I liked Elliott.

When I think of my dad twenty years later, what I remember most was his unconditional acceptance of me as a gay man in an unaccepting world, the classical music that was the background of our home, and the word *gratitude*.

This was my father's time and spirit—from my eyes, an authentic and transparent tribute.

THE END

APPENDICIES

Education

St. Pius School, Baltimore, Maryland, Diploma, Eighth Grade Grammar Course, Oblate Sisters of Providence, Sister C. M. Victoria, Principal, June 11, 1933.

Frederick Douglass Junior High Schools, Baltimore, Maryland, Certificate of Completion of Ninth Grade, David E. Weglein, Superintendent of Public Instruction, June 20, 1934.

Frederick Douglass High School, Athletic Certificate, Swimming, Alan A. Watty, Coach, Harry T. Pratt, May 29, 1936.

Frederick Douglass High School, Diploma, Academic Course, Harry T. Pratt, Principal, David E. Weglein, Superintendent of Public Instruction, June 21, 1937.

Cortez-Peters School, Commercial Courses in Business Administration, 21 months, 1938–1939.

National Radio Institute, Correspondence Course in Radio Practice and Theory, 18 months, 1947.

149

Employment

Alcazar Social Club, 1939–1941.

United States Army, Edgewood Arsenal, Chemical Plant Operator, February 1941 to January 1944.

United States Army, February 1944–1946.

United States Army, Edgewood Arsenal, Chemical Plant Operator, 1946–1971.

Appointed, Member of the Harford County Property Tax Assessment Appeal Board by Harry Hughes, Governor, The State of Maryland, February 17, 1981–1983.

Re-Appointment, Member of the Harford County Property Tax Assessment Appeal Board, by Harry Hughes, Governor, The State of Maryland, July 6, 1983–1988.

The Harford County Historical Society, Volunteer, 1986–2000.

Training Certificates

National Radio Institute, Radio Practice and Theory, Washington, DC, March 10, 1947.

De Forest's Training, Inc., Fundamentals of Electronics, Chicago, Illinois, July 11, 1951.

De Forest's Training, Inc., Radio Television and Servicing, Chicago, Illinois, May 13, 1952.

Foxboro Instruments, the Principles of Maintenance of Foxboro Instruments, Foxboro, Massachusetts, December 18, 1953.

Beckman Instruments, Fullerton, California, circa 1954.

Taylor Instruments, Rochester, New York, 1955.

Foxboro Instruments, The Advanced Principles of Maintenance of Foxboro Instruments, Foxboro, Massachusetts, July 26, 1957.

The Bristol Company, Bristol recorders, Controllers, and Telemetering Equipment, Waterbury, Connecticut, May 22, 1959.

Department of the Army Chemical Center and Chemical Corps Material Command, Introduction to Supervision, Army Chemical Center, Maryland, March 2, 1962.

Department of the Army Edgewood Arsenal, Supervisors Safety Training, Edgewood Arsenal, Maryland, February 8, 1963.

Sciaky Brothers, Inc., Chicago, London, Paris, Los Angeles, Dekatron Machine Theory and Maintenance, Chicago, Illinois, May 3, 1963.

COHU Electronics, Inc., Model 20/20 Television System, Kin Tel Division, San Diego, California, June 26, 1964.

Department of the Army Edgewood Arsenal, Effective Writing, Edgewood, Maryland, March 17, 1967.

Honeywell, Inc., Electronik 15, 18 Industrial Instrumentation, Philadelphia, Pennsylvania, December 10, 1969.

Department of the Army, Chemical Biological Surety Program Course for Supervisors, Edgewood Arsenal, Maryland, October 1970.

The Brotherhood of Man Gospel Choir, Certificate in Recognition for the Most Ambitious Member, September 15, 1974.

H&R Block, Certificate of Award, Basic Income Tax Preparation, December 15, 1977.

Military Records

Notice to Register to Appear for Physical Examination, Provident Hospital, 1514 Division Street, January 6, 1944.

Order to Report for Induction, Local Board #13 Baltimore City, 882 Park Avenue, January 29, 1944.

Fifth Training Regiment, Infantry Replacement Training Center, Fort McClellan, Alabama, Clerk-Typist, R. W. Scott, Major, Infantry, July 15, 1944.

United States of America Veteran's Administration, Certificate of Eligibility for Benefits of Title III of Servicemen's Readjustment Act of 1944.

Headquarters Infantry Replacement Training Center, Transfer Memorandum, Fort McClellan, Alabama, July 19, 1944.

Headquarters 49th Quartermaster Group APO 782 United States Army, Special Order, July 30, 1945.

Army of the United States, Honorable Discharge and Enlisted Record, Livorno, Italy, John T. McKee, Lieutenant Colonel, October 29, 1945.

Personnel Qualification Questionnaire, July 30, 1946.

Report for Physical Examination, Station Hospital Aberdeen Proving Ground, Maryland, August 5, 1946.

Ordnance Training Center, Letter of Qualification, Aberdeen Proving Ground, Maryland, August 16, 1946.

Ordnance Training Center, Transmittal of OCS Application, Aberdeen Proving Ground, Maryland, August 21, 1946.

Application for Enrollment in Officer Candidate School, Camp Lee Virginia, August 26, 1946.

War Department, The Adjutant General's Office, Washington, DC, September 16, 1946.

COD 9th Training Battalion Ordnance Training Center, Letter of Resubmission OCS, Aberdeen Proving Ground, Maryland, September 25, 1946.

RESTRICTED Ordnance Training Center, (Negro) Assigned to Overseas Replacement Depot, Camp Stoneman, California, October 9, 1946.

James R. Dorsey, Request Deletion from Orders, October 11, 1946.

James R. Dorsey, Request for Discharge, October 14, 1946.

Headquarters, Separation Detachment, San Francisco Port of Embarkation, Camp Stoneman, Pittsburg, California, December 12, 1946.

Army of the United States, Honorable Discharge and Separation Qualification Record, Camp Stoneman, California, December 13, 1946.

Veterans Administration, Training National Radio Institute, Baltimore, Maryland, March 10, 1947.

United States of America, Veterans Administration Certificate of Eligibility, Benefits of Title III of the Servicemen's Readjustment Act of 1944, November 8, 1954.

Memberships

Certificate of Membership, Order of Gregg Artists, Florence E. Ulrich, Chief Examiner, John R. Gregg, Author of Gregg Shorthand, circa 1938–1939.

Junior Membership, Order of Artistic Typist, Florence Ulrich, Membership Secretary, Harold H Smith, Editor, Gregg Typing, circa 1938-39.

President, Central Consolidated School, Parent Teacher Association (PTA), circa 1955.

Committee Chair for Investments, Vest Ten Investment Club, Inc., circa 1965.

Commander, American Legion Post 55, circa 1970.

Member, Toastmasters International, 1970–1976.

Acting President, Ross-Ruff Scholarship Fund, 1971–1975.

Member, Ames United Methodist Church, 1971–2000.

Tenor and Publicity Chair, Brotherhood of Man Gospel Choir, 1974–2000.

Harford Center Board of Directors, Appointed by Charles B. Anderson, Jr., County Executive, August 20, 1974.

Administrative Vice President, Toastmasters International, Gunpowder Club 2562, 1974–1975.

Treasurer and Trustee, Ames United Methodist Church, 1980–1989.

Records and History Committee, Ames United Methodist Church, April 1987–2000.

Secretary, the Mc Comas Institute Association, 1995–1998.

President, The Mc Comas Institute Association Incorporated, 1998–2000.

Awards

Certificate of Appreciation, State of Maryland, Armed Forces of the United States during World War II, Herbert R. O'Conor, Governor of Maryland, 1945.

Certificate of Service in Recognition of Twenty years of Federal Service, Department of the Army, June 30, 1961.

Officially Commended James R. Dorsey, Sr., for suggestion which was adopted by the federal government, United States Army, Paul R. Cerar, Colonel, Commanding, June 11, 1968.

Awarded to James R. Dorsey, Sr., "Better Product and Service at Reduced Cost", Frank G. White Major General, USA Commanding General United States Army Munitions Command, November 20, 1968.

Highest Honors in the Club Humorous Speech Contest, Toastmasters International, Gunpowder Toastmasters Club 2562-28, August 24, 1970.

Certificate in Recognition of Thirty Years of Federal Service, The Department of the Army, May 5, 1971.

Certificate in Recognition of Outstanding Cooperation and Support, Medical Eye Bank of Maryland, Inc., July 14, 1971.

Certificate of Appreciation, John K. Stoner, Jr. Colonel, Commanding Edgewood Arsenal, the Department of the Army, April 1, 1972.

Certificate of Retirement from Federal Service Under the Provisions of the Civil Service Retirement Act, John K. Stoner, Jr., Colonel, Commanding Edgewood Arsenal, The Department of the Army, August 11, 1972.

Second Highest Honors in the Area of Humorous Speech Contest, Toastmasters International, Gunpowder Toastmasters Club 2562, September 30, 1972.

Certification of Progress, Communications and Leadership Program, Section 1, Toastmasters International, January 15, 1974.

Certified Lay Speaker Certificate, Ames United Methodist Church, 1974.

Advanced Lay Speaker, Baltimore East District, School of Discipleship, October 1983.

James Roswell Dorsey, Sr., First Recipient of the George B. Gwynn Christian Service Award, Biography Written by Wife, Zelma Virginia Curry Dorsey, 1983.

Certificate of Appreciation, Sunday School Teacher, Church School, Adults, Ames United Methodist Church, September 1987.

Official Citation, Recognition of Service, Zeta Phi Beta Sorority, Inc., Omicron Chi Zeta Chapter and the Harford County Community, Presented by the Senators and Delegates of Harford Country, October 27, 1996.

Recognition of Outstanding Service on Behalf of Your Community and Volunteer Work and Humanitarian Endeavors, The State of Maryland, Parris N. Glendening, Governor, October 27, 1996.

Certificate of Appreciation in Recognition of Black History Month, Department of Veteran's Affairs, Wilmington, Delaware Vet Center, February 21, 1997.

Certificate of Appreciation in Recognition of Service Rendered to Our Country, Veteran's Day November 10, 2000 Wilmington, Delaware Vet Center, Department of Veteran's Affairs, presented October 29, 2000.

2000 Preservationist Award, James Dorsey, Harford County Historic Preservation Commission, James M. Harkins, Harford County Executive and W. Paul Thompson, Jr. Chair Historic Preservation Commission, 2000.

I Get Around, Take a trip back in time at the Mc Comas Institute, by Karen Toussaint, The Aegis, Bel Air, Maryland, February 17, 1999.

Harford residents, preserve history, natural beauty, by Karen Toussaint, The Aegis, Bel Air, Maryland, May 19, 2000.

African American History of Harford County Project (AAHHCP), Pamphlet 0025 and 0026, by Maurice W. Dorsey, PhD, June 24, 2016.

African American History of Harford County Project (AAHHCP), Pamphlet 0113, April 5, 2019.

Letters

Letter of Support from Donald P. Smith, Major, Headquarters Edgewood Arsenal, Chemical Warfare Service, January 29, 1944.

Letter of Reference from John Tooker, Plant Supervisor, Chemical Warfare Service, October 6, 1944.

Letter Appreciation, Executive Department, Annapolis, Maryland, J. Millard Taws, Governor, November 23, 1960.

Letter of Appreciation, George D. Sisson, Jr., Colonel, Director of Manufacturing Technology, June 15, 1972.

Personal Letter, Percy V. Williams, Assistant State Superintendent Division of Compensatory, Urban, and Supplementary Programs, Maryland State Department of Education, BWI Airport, Baltimore, Maryland, June 25, 1975.

Letter of Appreciation from Kenneth T. Gill, Principal, Magnolia Middle School, Afro American History Month Presentation, Joppa, Maryland, February 27, 1980.

Personal Letter, from James Roswell Dorsey, Sr. to Maurice W. Dorsey, March 24, 1999.

Letter of Notification from Harford County Historic Preservation Commission to James R. Dorsey, Sr., Unanimously Voted 2000 Historic Preservationist Award (Margaret D. Pagan, daughter accepted for her late father), April 21, 2000.

Photographs

James R. Dorsey, Sr., Military Uniform, circa 1944.

James R. Dorsey, Sr., At Sea, circa 1945.

James R. Dorsey, Sr., Sitting Outside of the Barracks, circa 1945.

James R. Dorsey, Sr., Walking on Howard Street home after Army Discharge, December 1946.

Carrie Elizabeth Snowden-Dorsey (Mother) and James R. Dorsey, Sr., Sipping Cocktails circa 1946.

Foxboro Training Class, Foxboro, Massachusetts, December 1, 1953.

Taylor Instruments, Training Class, Rochester, New York, September 1955.

Foxboro Training Class, Foxboro, Massachusetts, July 9, 1957.

Honeywell, Inc. Training Class, Philadelphia Division, December 10, 1968.

Thirty Years of Federal Service Group, May 27, 1971.

National Association for the Advancement of Colored People, Harford County Chapter, Picnic, 1973.

Retirement Party for Pringle, Edgewood Arsenal, 1971.

Margaret D. Pagan, daughter, accepted 2000 Preservationist Award for her late father, May 16, 2000.

Other References

Conditional Sale Contract, Anderson Used Cars, Inc., April 25, 1949.

Certified Certificate of Birth, Health Department of Baltimore City, Pinkney McCready, State Registrar of Vital Records, Given Name: James Roswell Dorsey, Added January 29, 1968, Issued May 18, 1979.

Holland America Cruises, Sailing from New York, July 28, 1973.

James Roswell Dorsey, Sr., First Recipient of the George B. Gwynn Christian Service Award, Biography written by Zelma V. Dorsey.

Mc Comas Institute Association's Dedication Service for the renovation, Mc Comas Institute, Freedmen's School Established 1867 Renovated 1995, Harford County Maryland, September 23, 1995.

Consecration Sunday, Ames United Methodist Church, May 12, 2002.

Sanctuary Rededication, Ames United Methodist Church, Sunday, May 15, 2016.

141st Anniversary Homecoming Worship Service, Ames United Methodist Church, October 8, 2017.

Personal Conversations with James Roswell Dorsey, Sr.

Personal Conversations with Zelma Virginia Dorsey.

Certificate of Death, State Registrar of Vital Records, Issued December 6, 2000.

BIBLIOGRAPHY

Publications

James R. Dorsey, Sr., "Men at War, Edgewood Arsenal, Maryland 1918," *Harford Historical Bulletin* No.27, p. 18–23, Winter 1986.

James R. Dorsey, Sr., "Religion: Convictions Run Deep," February 1, 1995.

President's Newsletter, the McComas Institute Association, Inc., Who Are We? and President's Message, 1915 Singer Road, Joppa, Maryland 21085, Volume 7 Number 1, March 1998.

President's Newsletter, the McComas Institute Association, Inc., 1915 Singer Road, Joppa, Maryland 21085, Volume 7 Number 2, June 1998.

Newspaper Clippings

Notices, Edgewood Arsenal Weapons Development and Engineering Laboratories, presented to James Dorsey, $590 for suggesting an improved system for detecting leaks, the *Aegis*, June 1968.

"Makes Roll, of economic champions in the Pentagon." The *Aegis*, Bel Air, Maryland, circa 1968.

"Toastmasters Guest Day and Founders Day Program Welcomes New Members." The *Aegis*, Bel Air, Maryland, circa 1968.

Biography James R. Dorsey, Sr. The *Aegis*, Bel Air, Maryland, March 21, 1974.

Board of Education of Harford County, B-Line, Board Meeting Public Testimony. Bel Air, Maryland, April 12, 1977.

Harford County, Maryland. "Harris Resigns from Property Tax Appeal Board." The *Aegis*, Bel Air, Maryland, March 12, 1981.

Harford County, Maryland, "Council Accepts 3 Names for Local Tax Appeal Board." The *Aegis*, Bel Air, Maryland, April 23, 1981.

Your Government in Harford County. "James R. Dorsey, Sr., First Black to Ever Hold Seat on the Board. The *Aegis*, Bel Air, Maryland, June 9, 1983.

Your Government in Harford County. "James R. Dorsey, Sr., Will Serve a Five-Year Term." The *Aegis*, Bel Air, Maryland, July 14, 1983.

"'Ros' Dorsey Helps Compile History of Blacks in Harford" by Don Morrison. The *Aegis*, Bel Air, Maryland, May 15, 1986.

National Association for the Advancement of Colored People (NAACP) Newsletter, Profile: James R. Dorsey, Sr., by Margaret Pagan, Writer/Editor, Social Security Administration, October 1989.

Black History: Events, programs set to note social impact, by Ben Keenan. The *Record*, Havre De Grace, Maryland, January 31, 1990.

African American History of Harford County, Maryland, Rescuing McComas Institute, Pamphlet 0113, April 5, 2019.

The *Baltimore Sun*. 100 Years of Making Suits Hass: Now a Century Old, Hass Tailoring Co. is still looking to the future even as it recalls with pride some of the famous who have purchased its made-in-Baltimore suits. By Sean Somerville, April 21, 1997.

Wikipedia. Good Friday.

Wikipedia. Edgewood Arsenal human experiments.

Wikipedia. European-African-Middle Eastern Campaign Medal.

Wikipedia. *The Razor's Edge.*

Wikipedia. W. Somerset Maugham.

Wikipedia. *Manhattan Tower* (Gordon Jenkins Album).

Wikipedia. *My Fair Lady* (Broadway Cast Recording).

Wikipedia. *The King and I* (1956 film).

Wikipedia, *The Sound of Music* (film).

Wikipedia, Hecht's.

Wikipedia, Hochschild Kohn's.

Wikipedia, Stewart's Department Store.

Wikipedia, John F. Kennedy.

Wikipedia, The John Carroll School.

Wikipedia, Hutzler's.

Wikipedia, Vietnam War.

Wikipedia, Phil Donahue.

Wikipedia, Enoch Pratt Free Library.

INDEX

A

Aberdeen Proving Ground, 33–35, 152–53

Adams, Victorine, 21

Aegis, 104, 122, 126–27, 130, 135, 141, 144, 156, 161–62

Agnes (aunt), 21–22, 39

Ames United Methodist Church, xxi, 1, 115–16, 123–24, 128–29, 133–34, 144, 147, 154–56, 159

Anderson, Charles B., Jr., 123, 154

apartment, 9

15-B Hartman Street, 24

18 Battle Street, 24–25

20 Battle Street, 40–41, 51–52

129-F Hawthorne Drive, 51

Maurice's, 110–11, 113

Army Chemical Center, xx, xxiii, 23, 37, 50, 54, 88, 151

Army of Occupation Medal, 32–33

Austin, Gendolyn Hackley, 134

B

Baltimore City Public School System, 111

beaches, 94, 111

Beckman Instruments, 50

Bel Air High School, ix, 93–94, 96

bird of paradise, 94

birth control, 15, 23

Black History Month, 134–35, 140, 156

blacks, 93–94, 135–38

free, 136–37

history of, xxi, 129–30, 133–34, 138, 144–45, 162

black students, 89, 106–7

Bramble, Forrest, 19

Bristow, Andy, xxi

Broadway, 7–8, 61, 130

Brotherhood of Man Gospel Choir, 123, 151, 154

Brown, R. T., 37

Brown v. the Board of Education, 92, 125

Brynner, Yul, 62

Bunker, Archie, 105

165

C

Camp Shelby, 29
Camp Stoneman, 35–36, 153
career, xx–xxii, 20, 23, 36–38, 47, 69, 124, 144
Carroll, John, 93, 163
Carr's Beach, 94
casino, 8–9, 142
Catholic Church, xix, 12, 14–15, 37, 55, 58–59, 87, 114–16, 131
rituals of, 44
Catholic church, segregated, xvi, xx, 138, 147
Catholic Church indoctrination, 14, 131
Catholic Church law, 13–14, 45, 114
Catholicism, xxi, 16, 50, 58–59, 115
Catholic Schools, xx, 13, 15, 18, 22, 58
Central Consolidated School, 74, 83, 92, 122, 124, 153
charities, 117
Chief. *See* Edward (Dad's brother)
children, raising, 60, 91, 102
chores, 43, 81, 96, 144
Christmas, 15, 47, 78, 107, 144
Christmastime, 46–47, 77
Christmas tree, 77–78
church, black, 125, 137
Civil Rights Act of 1964, 125
Clark (neighbor), 91
Colored High and Training School. *See* Frederick Douglass High School
coloreds, 27, 34, 44, 138
communication, xiii–xiv, 35, 92, 131–32
confessions, 14, 38, 53, 59, 119

construction, house, 76, 79
Cortez Peters Business School, 20, 28, 30, 48, 86, 141
Cushman, Joseph W., 33

D

Dad
army life, xx, 26–32
baptism of, xix
birth of, 12
childhood of, 26, 58, 63, 80
confession to Mom, 37
culture of, 61–68
death of, xxii, 10, 144
discharge from army, 36
discovering passion in life, xxii, 129
family of, 12
funeral of, 1–145
and golf, 71
grandparents of, 14
heart attacks, xxi, 3–4, 6, 9, 102, 115, 144, 148
high school graduation, 19
honorable discharge, 35
jokes of, xviii, 68–69, 76, 112, 132
journal entries of, 15, 21, 29–30, 131
leg injury, 38–39
life of, xxii
love of poetry, 10, 16–17
love of records, 63
marriage of, 22
"Men at War, Edgewood Arsenal, Maryland 1918," *130*, 161
in old age, 9
parents of, 13–14, 54
poems by, 70, 134
on punctuality, xix, 8, 92
reading habit, 16, 63–66
reenlistment of, 32

religious beliefs of, 14, 23, 44, 58, 133
retirement of, 6, 115–17
schools attended, xix, 15, 19
sense of humor, xvii, 68, 112
on sexuality, 87
start of drinking, 15
thank-you letter from, 29, 142
training courses of, xxiii–xxiv, 37, 49, 92, 98, 100, 108, 112, 126
Darrell, Larry, 63–64, 75
Department of the Army, xxiv–xxv, 87, 98, 104, 112, 115, 151, 154–55
division chief, 88
Donahue, Phil, 133, 163
Dorsey, Carrie Elizabeth Snowden. *See* grandmother
Dorsey, James Rosell, Sr., xix, 31, 104, 123, 134, 141, 143
Dorsey, Leander Edward. *See* grandfather

E

EAME Medal, 30
Edgewood Arsenal, 6, 23, 26, 31, 33, 35, 43, 48, 56, 71, 74, 98, 104, 113, 130–31
Edward (Dad's brother), 13, 16–17, 19
emotions, xiv, 2–3, 7, 51, 132
English Racer, 73
Enoch Pratt Free Library, ix, 65, 80, 163
Eva (Dad's girlfriend), 21–22

F

Fitzgerald, Ella, 61, 66
flowers, 2, 94, 134
Forest Hill, 78, 93, 96, 121

Fort George G. Meade, 31
Fort Holabird, 97, 103
Fort McClellan, 27–28, 30, 152
Foxboro Instruments, xxiii–xxiv, 48–50, 150–51
Frederick Douglass High School, 19, 30
Freedmen's Bureau, 138–39, 141

G

Gauguin, Paul, xviii, 66
General Motors, 53
gin, xviii, 3–4, 15, 113, 145, 147
drinking, 47, 82, 113, 127–28
Glendening, Paris N., 139
Glenn L. Martin Company, 23
grandfather (of Maurice), xix, 12–14, 55
grandmother (of Maurice), xix, 12–14, 17, 22, 39, 54–56, 65, 127–28, 158
Great Depression, 12, 15, 19, 64

H

Harford Center Board, 123
Harford County, xxi–xxii, xxv, 75, 84, 87, 92–93, 95, 117, 123–27, 130, 133–39, 143, 150, 156–59, 162
Harford County Board of Education, 125, 139
Harford County Historical Society, xxi–xxii, 130, 134, 150
Harford County Property Tax Assessment Board, 126
Harford Historical Bulletin, 130, 161
Harrell, Henry, 21–22
Hass Tailoring Company, 13

Havre de Grace Consolidated School, 91
Hecht's, 46–47, 163
Hickory Hills, 78, 91
Historic Preservation Award, 145
history, 138
    African American, xxi–xxii, 130, 145, 148, 156, 162
    of church, 136
Hogue, Richard, 127
homeownership, 9, 52, 76, 79, 99
Honeywell, Inc., 108
Hughes, Harry, 126, 150
Hutzler's Men's Department, 98

I

independence, 6, 91, 109–10
injustices, 89, 138
integration, 6, 92–93
Interpace Construction, 101

J

John Carroll School, 93, 163

K

Keenan, Ben, 134, 162
Kelly, Sharon Pratt, 124
Kennedy, John Fitzgerald, 85, 89, 163
    Profiles in Courage, 85
Kerr, Deborah, 62
King, Eric W., Sr., 10, 144
The King and I, 61–63, 163
Klu Klux Klan, 125
Knowles, Edward M., 56

L

La Cage aux Follies, 7–8, 65
Little Willie, 21
Loch Raven VA Medical Center, 9

M

Macbeth (Shakespeare), 16–17
Madison Avenue Presbyterian Church, xix, 14
marriage, xiii, xx, 13–14, 22–23, 25, 43, 50, 57, 65, 70, 96, 115, 129, 133, 144
masturbation, xix, 22–23, 133
maturity, xv, 92
Maugham, W. Somerset, xviii, 63, 65–66, 141, 148, 163
    The Moon and Sixpence, 66
    The Razor's Edge, 63
Maurice
    childhood of, xiii–xiv, xix, 48, 53, 63, 74, 78, 101, 105
    coming out, 118
    graduation of, 108
    junior year in college, 105
    spending money, 89, 106
Maurice (uncle), 39
McComas Institute Association, 139–40, 161
McGee, Mel, 122
Mester, Edmund C., 84
Michael (Edward's son), 19
military, xvii, 19, 25, 27, 29, 36, 58, 60, 93, 97, 114, 116
Miss Dot, 101
Mom, 1–6, 9–10, 41, 47–48, 51, 53–57, 67, 69–73, 75–77, 80–83, 86–88, 96–99, 102–3, 105–7, 113–21
    birthing Maurice, 38–40
    on Dad's reenlistment, 32
    on debt and money, 42–43, 96
    fashion of, 67
    on home ownership, 52
    marriage, 21–22, 25
    religious beliefs, 43–44, 58, 115
    on sex, 38

Mom, Maurice's disagreement with, 82

Moon and Sixpence, The (Gauguin), 66

Moore, John W., 32

Morrison, Don, 130, 162

Mount Zion Meeting House, 136

Mount Zion Methodist Church, 139

music, xviii, 7–8, 28, 61–63, 74, 76, 116, 145, 163

My Fair Lady, 62

N

National Advancement of Colored People (NAACP), xxi, 122, 133, 162

National Guard Armory, 91

National Radio Institute, 37, 149–50, 153

NCAA Basketball Tournament, 106

Negros, 6, 34, 47–49, 53, 71, 80, 84, 87, 94, 138

New York City, 62

Nottage, Thomas. *See* Tommy (Dad's best friend)

nuns, xix, 13, 15–16, 18, 65

nursing homes, 9, 143

Nutcracker Suite, 61

O

Oblate Sisters of Providence, 13, 149

Officer Candidate School (OCS), xvii, xx, 33, 35, 37

Ordnance Training Center, 34–35, 152–53

Overture to Tannhauser, 7

P

Pagan, Margaret, 133, 162

Paige, Robert, 74

Parent-Teacher Association (PTA), xxi, 46, 74, 83, 122, 125, 153

pawnshop, 86–87

Pearl Harbor, 24–25, 140

Pennsylvania Avenue, 86

Peters, Cortez, Sr., 20

Peters, Cortez W., Jr., 124

Phil Donahue Show, 133

Pratt, Harry T., 18–19, 149

Profiles in Courage (Kennedy), 85

Provident Hospital, 27, 38, 152

public schools, xix–xx, 18, 27, 31, 92, 124, 130, 138

R

racial discrimination, xx, 125

racism, xx, 26, 28, 93, 115, 125, 138

incidents of, 28

Razor's Edge, The (Maugham), xviii, 63–64, 66, 75, 148, 163

Rehabilitation and Extended Care Center, 143

Rehoboth Beach, 94

"Religion: Convictions Run Deep" (Dorsey), xxv, 135

Rimsky-Korsakov, Nikolai, 61

Rogers, Richard, 63

Roosevelt, Franklin D., 30

Rosalie (Dad's sister), xiv, xix, 20, 42, 100, 127–28, 139

Ross, Robert E. Lee, 94

S

Saint Emma's Military Academy, 25–26, 96
Sandy Point, 94
school
segregated, 78, 91
white, 92–93, 108, 148
segregation, xx, 26–27, 30, 36, 44, 79, 87, 115–16, 138
Sensenbaugh, James A., 124
Shakespeare, William, 10, 16, 28
Macbeth, 16
Sisters of the Blessed Sacrament, 19
slavery, 51, 135–37
slaves, 113, 136–38
Smedley, Ralph C., 112
Smith, Donald, 26
Smith, Harold H., 20
Smith Corona typewriter, 85–86
"Sound of Music, The," 61, 63, 163
St. Barnabas Catholic Church, 14
St. Emma's Military Academy, xix, 19–20, 37, 57
Swan Lake, 61

T

Tawers, J. Millard, 83
Tax Appeal Board, 126, 162
Taylor Instruments, xxiv, 50, 151, 158
Templeton, Elliott, 64–65
Theresa (aunt), 39
Toastmasters Club, 155
Toastmasters International, xxi, 112, 122, 133, 154–55, 161
Tommy (Dad's best friend), 61, 99–100
Tooker, John, 31, 157

Toussaint, Karen, 141, 144, 156
Truman, Harry S., 36
Turner, Ray, 36

U

Ulrich, Florence E., 20, 153
United Methodist Church Conference, 124
United States Army, segregated, 26
United States Army Intelligence School and Counter-intelligence Records Facility, 97
University of Maryland, 3, 86, 96–97, 101–3, 106, 108, 148
University of Maryland-College Park, 96, 102
University of Maryland Placement Office, 109

V

Veterans Medical Center, 143
Vietnam War, 97, 103, 108, 163

W

Watters Methodist Meeting House, 136
Weekly Reader, 53
Weeks, Christopher, 143
Weglein, David E., 19, 149
Williams, Percy V., 124–25, 139, 157
Willie (Mom's aunt), 21
Willis, John T., 139
Winfrey, Oprah, 133
Wolfe, Charles E., 127
Woods, Eleanor, 113, 120–21

Woods, George, 13, 31, 113, 119–21, 128, 156–58
World War I, 63, 130
World War II, xx, 19, 32, 74, 143, 154
Wright, James T., 35

Y

Young Men's Christian Association (YMCA), xx, 20, 30, 112

Z

Zelma (*see also* Mom), xxiii, 21–22, 45, 47, 67, 70, 81–82, 103, 119, 156, 158–59